Mental Disorder and Community Safety

Also by Philip Bean:

Compulsory Admissions to Mental Hospitals
Mental Disorder and Legal Control
Discharged from Mental Hospitals* (with P. Mounser)

Also published by Palgrave

Mental Disorder and Community Safety

Philip Bean

Consultant editor: Jo Campling

palgrave

First published 2001 by
PALGRAVE
Houndmills, Basingstoke, Hampshire RG21 6XS and
175 Fifth Avenue, New York, N.Y. 10010
Companies and representatives throughout the world

PALGRAVE is the new global academic imprint of
St. Martin's Press LLC Scholarly and Reference Division and
Palgrave Publishers Ltd (formerly Macmillan Press Ltd).

ISBN 0–333–61871–8

This book is printed on paper suitable for recycling and made from fully managed and sustained forest sources.

A catalogue record for this book is available from the British Library.

10 9 8 7 6 5 4 3 2 1
10 09 08 07 06 05 04 03 02 01

Printed in Malaysia

For
Laurence and Cianna-Fae

Contents

Preface

Since the 1983 Mental Health Act came into operation in England and Wales, unprecedented changes have taken place, the most important being that mental hospitals are no longer the centre of the mental health services. The emphasis now is on community care, or at least it was until community safety became the current watchword. As a result, new questions have arisen, and new debates generated, yet many older questions remain. Who should be responsible for detaining patients under compulsion? How should mentally disordered offenders be dealt with in police stations? How should the rights of the mentally disordered be protected? Linking the old with the new has been one aim of this book, for the old questions are no less important, having a timeless quality about them.

No single book on mental disorder can cover all its aspects, and this book is no exception. I have not, for example, dealt with sentencing the mentally disordered, or with the special hospitals, except obliquely. Rather, I have aimed to cover those areas which centre around community safety, and which incidentally also happen to include aspects with which I am more familiar. In this sense, the book has become more of a personal narrative than perhaps it ought. It follows from three earlier books: *Compulsory Admissions to Mental Hospitals* (1980) published by John Wiley, which was a study on the way patients were compulsorily admitted under what was then the 1959 Mental Health Act; *Mental Disorder and Legal Control* (1987) published by Cambridge University Press, which was a collection of essays on the 1983 Mental Health Act; and *Discharged from Mental Hospitals* (1992), written with Patricia Mounser and published by Macmillan, which explored the implications of the decarceration movement on patients discharged from hospital. This present book has a slightly different aim, which is to consider some implications of the changing social climate and the emerging themes of the 2000s as well as taking into account the recent government proposals for changing the 1983 Mental Health Act.

Many friends and colleagues will recognise their contribution to this book. They may remember those lengthy debates, often initiated unashamedly as a means of clarifying some ideas besetting a study of this nature, whether about treatability, the Appropriate Adult, diversion or the activities of police surgeons. Those who have contributed are too numerous to mention but include my colleagues at the Midlands Centre for Criminology, Loughborough University, Louis Blom-Cooper, Teresa Nemitz, Judith Pitchers, Herschel Prins and Jon Vagg. Sally Weston and William Bingley kindly read the drafts and made valuable comments for which I thank them. Needless to say the errors that remain are mine, as are the interpretations of those debates and comments. My thanks also to Jo Campling and the staff at Palgrave for their patience throughout.

My family gave more assistance than I could reasonably expect. A special mention must be given to my wife Valerie, whose tragic and untimely death in the week or so before the book was completed has left its permanent mark. I wish to acknowledge the help given by our many friends who gave such comfort and support during that time; they provided and continue to provide more than anyone should reasonably expect. Also, I want to acknowledge our two sons, Ian and Lee. That this book is dedicated to two of our grandchildren is a further indication of the importance I give to my family, and my indebtedness to them.

Deirdre Lombard typed the manuscript in her usual efficient way. To her and to the others in the Department of Social Sciences at Loughborough University I acknowledge help and assistance.

PHILIP BEAN

1

Introduction: Community Safety and Mental Disorder

The question to be asked is this: how, in an age when community safety is dominant, can we retain the integrity of mental health? By integrity I mean how can we care for the mentally disordered when the tendency is to control, punish and regard them with increasing suspicion. The mentally disordered are a common sight in every large city. Some may be homeless, some may be substance abusers, and a small number may be violent, with an even smaller number involved in high-profile fatalities. Their high levels of visibility help to promote a sense of unease, assisted, of course, by the media and the shrill response of some pressure groups.

To what extent can mental health law solve these problems? What is it able to do about them, or rather what is that part of mental health law which is concerned with compulsory detention able to do about them? On the face of it, the answer seems very little, for rarely have we improved matters, and sometimes we have made them worse. Mental health law is not, it seems, geared up to solve such problems. Clearly, patients who are a danger to others can, and presumably will, be detained in hospital, but the numbers involved will be small, producing little effect on levels of community safety. Commitment laws are permissive, not mandatory – eligible patients cannot be hospitalised even if they meet the commitment criteria, for they are admitted at the discretion and direction of the clinician (Appelbaum 1994, p. 51). Moreover, levels of commitment may be related more to available facilities than to demands for protection, that is, to the numbers of beds, where the length of stay is also related to pressure to produce a high turnover of patients, and so on. These and other examples in the text point to the limitations of mental health law as a means of solving social problems – a lesson we have still to learn.

Demands for public safety (the terms 'community safety' and 'public safety' will be used interchangeably) are entirely legitimate and have to be taken seriously. It will not do, as with some mental health specialists, to see public safety as an overreaction, itself created by the media. Whenever and wherever there are public or private confrontations with the mentally disordered they are never pleasant, and may often be frightening. As well as the current high level of fear of crime, there is suspicion, anger, disbelief and exasperation that such patients are given free rein to intimidate others. Demands for more controls become an understandable response. One aim of this book is to explore the nature of some of those demands and see to what extent existing controls are adequate and whether new ones are required.

A brief and cursory examination of those currently in existence shows how difficult and complex the matter is. The direction in which things are moving is rarely clear, and the pattern, if there is one, is difficult to determine. Community safety can be promoted on the one hand yet denied or opposed on the other. For example, Supervision Registers and community supervision were introduced to provide additional controls (never mind for the moment questions of their effectiveness), while at the same time, and at the other extreme, diversion remains central to government policy. Or again, there are concerns about potentially dangerous mentally disordered offenders, but there are government requests that police stations are not to be used as a place of safety for the mentally disordered found in a public place, some of whom may be offenders. Nor is there any uniformity about patients' rights; while there are legitimate concerns about furthering consent to treatment, there are few on the rights of mental patients in police stations.

Determining the integrity of mental health means providing appropriate facilities and services. Mentally disordered patients have a right, as do the somatically disordered, to receive treatment. The tricky questions are where is that to be, and who is to give it? Mentally disordered patients may also be offenders, and in drawing attention to this I am not concerned with aetiology, or the links between mental disorder and crime, I am simply saying that this is so. It has been government policy to remove offender patients from the criminal justice system and treat them through the mainstream psychiatric services, whether before or after sentence. As will be shown later, the position adopted in this book is to suggest that this is not the way to secure the integrity of mental health, rather it is to sentimentalise and excuse their offending.

Irrespective of the route by which we have arrived at this position or the justification for it, there have been increasing demands for community safety. These are not new, they have simply reappeared in a different form. We seem to move as if in a cyclical model, going from one control system to another. When each is tried and failed, we move to the next, yet, without realising it, find ourselves travelling in a circle, finally returning to the point from which we started. (This in contrast to the so-called pendulum model of mental health legislation so favoured by Jones (1960) where legislation is seen to swing from one extreme to the other.) Community care was tried in the 18th century and found not to work. Mental hospitals were introduced, but these too were found not to work, leading to new forms of community care. These in turn were seen as expensive failures, so now in the 21st century we are moving back to a more institutional approach dominated by new-style hospitals, this time to be called secure units, but essentially the same as before (see Bean and Mounser 1993).

This is an oversimplification of course; the community care programmes of the 18th century bore little resemblance to those of the 1980s and 90s, but even so there is an underlying grain of truth about the cyclical model of care. Community care in its most fashionable form was an ideology which assumed it was desirable for mental patients to live independently, take responsibility for themselves, and adapt to the demands and rigours of life outside the mental hospital. In its purist form it meant keeping psychiatric patients out of institutions, with expanding community services to enable patients to remain in the community. It was not difficult to predict what would happen; closing the mental hospitals and replacing them with a system of community care seemed wonderfully progressive, but what of those patients unable to cope outside the hospital? Inevitably, they produced demands for more community controls.

A series of high-profile fatalities have fostered those demands – especially those which involved attacks on strangers, or where multiple fatalities involved the offender's family – backed by official inquiries which described the patients' living conditions as worse than those in the mental hospital. No doubt the debate will continue; questions will be asked about whether community care was intrinsically flawed, or whether its failure was due to a lack of resources. Whatever the answers, these high-profile cases have helped to promote demands for community safety, and, by implication, have condemned community care. The statement by the Health Secretary, Frank Dobson, in July 1998, added to the criticisms:

Care in the community has failed. Discharging people from institutions has brought benefits to some. But it has left many vulnerable patients trying to cope on their own. Others have been left to become a danger to themselves and a nuisance to others. Too many confused and sick people have been left wandering the streets and sleeping rough. A small but significant minority has become a danger to the public as well as themselves. (Department of Health press release 1998a)

It is not the aim here to examine why community care has failed – if indeed it has – but to accept that community safety is one of the features it has brought in its wake. Caring for and controlling the mentally disordered under community care has produced new control programmes, while some older forms have been retained, inherited from earlier legislation. They will be considered alongside recent developments. The problems of dual diagnosis, or dual disorder as it is sometimes called, are included in Chapter 8.

An overview of the legislation

One occupational group dominates the control system, the psychiatrists, aided by the police, nurses, social workers and psychologists – the latter having a less formal role to play. All are backed by the resources of the NHS and by the criminal justice system. Mental health legislation is now an accepted part of the state control apparatus – it seems odd that there were once disagreements about whether legislation, which required patients to receive treatment against their will, should be regarded as coercive. Civil commitment, often called involuntary commitment, has been defined by one commentator as 'the most serious deprivation of liberty that a society may impose' (quoted in Hoyer 1999). Compared with the frequent and extensive justifications provided for detention in the criminal justice system, 'no such intellectual effort has been directed at providing justification for societal use of civil commitment procedures' (quoted in Hoyer 1999). Georg Hoyer makes the point that, although the above statement was made 30 years ago, the situation has not improved much since then.

> Taking into consideration the seriousness of the questions involved, and the large proportion of persons who are subject to the use of coercion in the mental health system, it is surprising how little attention is paid to this vital problem. (ibid.)

There have of course been exceptions, but Georg Hoyer's point is largely correct; little attention has been paid, and control is an accepted part of mental health.

The term 'control' is not used here in a pejorative sense. By control I mean those organised responses, which may be reactive, that is, after the mental disorder has arisen and the patient been identified, or proactive, that is, in order to prevent the disorders occurring (although in practice there are few proactive measures in mental health). Organised responses may be sponsored by the state or by autonomous professional bodies such as psychiatrists and social workers. Following Stanley Cohen (1985, p. 3), the goals might be specific to individual treatments, or be diffuse to include mental health policy. Here, I am interested in how the mentally disordered are controlled in the community, how controls are introduced, and the plans, if any, for the future, although such plans as there are will be fairly disparate and likely to include a ragbag of topics centring around a set of key assumptions – themselves difficult to determine.

The main legislation is the 1983 Mental Health Act (referred to hereafter as the 1983 Act). It is wide-ranging but not comprehensive; that is to say, it does not include all relevant mental health legislation in England and Wales. Its scope and boundaries are subject to change. For these purposes the 1983 Act provides the central focus, although only a small number of topics covered by the Act are included here. Other topics not covered by the Act have been included, for example the uses of Appropriate Adults are dealt with by the Codes of Practice under the Police and Criminal Evidence Act (PACE) 1984 and not the Mental Health Act 1983. Under the Codes, decisions are made within the police station about whether a suspect becomes a patient or an offender; that is, whether he finishes up in the mental health rather than the criminal justice system. The duties of the Forensic Medical Examiners (FMEs), police surgeons as they used to be called, are also not included in the 1983 Act, yet FMEs are able to define and redefine the suspect's position as being within criminal justice or mental health. So, if and when they identify suspects as mentally disordered, the suspect will be transferred out of the criminal justice system into the mental health system, and if not, the suspect enters the criminal justice system as before. The duties of the FME have a decisive impact on decisions about the mentally disordered.

The Act itself is lengthy and complex: it includes *inter alia* powers to deal with mentally disordered offenders, before and after sentence; to transfer prisoners to and from prisons and special hospitals; and for consent to treatment provisions for civil patients. What is and what is not included in the Act can only be explained by reference to legal precedents, earlier legislation and decisions by Parliament. Supervised Discharge Orders are in the Mental Health (Patients in the Community)

Act 1995, details on Supervision Registers are entirely administrative procedures and can be found in the Health Service Guidelines HSG(94)5 (Department of Health 1994), which build on earlier Guidelines set out in the Introduction of the Care Programme Approach (Department of Health 1990). Matters relating to the insanity defences are found elsewhere.

The authority for civil commitment is found in the 1983 Mental Health Act, mainly under Sections 2, 3 and 4. Briefly, these sections provide powers for physicians to make the recommendations, and for social workers and relatives to make the applications – recommendations and applications are required before the patient is admitted. The civil commitment procedures are supplemented under additional powers to detain patients suspected of being mentally disordered in a public place. Section 136 of the 1983 Mental Health Act allows a police constable to take a patient to a place of safety in order to be examined by a physician and social worker.

The variety of topics included in the legislation reflects an increasingly sophisticated mental health and criminal justice system. The various occupational groups involved – psychiatrists, social workers, police and so on – are required to work together, but retain their own professional interests. As expected, these various groups may work together for the benefit of the whole, but just as easily may help to protect their own empires. Separating the various strands of the debate, distinguishing between sectional vested interests and identifying those acting in a benevolent way is far from easy. What follows is an attempt to pull out some features of the debate, reviewing and reflecting upon some of the controversies.

Mental health legislation: some theoretical features

In her Introduction to *Mental Health Law* (1984), Brenda Hoggett says 'Mental health law serves a mass of conflicting interests and ideologies'. She also says that mental health law often produces suspicion, for it appears to offer too readily an excuse for criminal behaviour. She added somewhat darkly that the consequences of this could be as severe for the patients entering the psychiatric system as for those entering the criminal justice system.

There have been numerous debates and discussions about what should be the aim of mental health legislation: should it assist patients to receive treatment, and if so, should it enable those professionals involved to provide a service with the minimum of hindrance to themselves and the patient? Or should it set standards and boundaries which professionals must respect, and provide a framework of powers for the detention of the mentally disordered, whether in hospital or elsewhere? In Chapter 2, some of these questions are touched upon when considering the justification for compulsory powers, but here I want to look at a different set of questions. What is it about mental health law that sets it apart from other laws, or rather, how does it fit into and be part of the general context of law? That is, should mental health law be seen as separate or as a subsection of law generally, and if so in what way?

In an earlier publication (Bean 1980), I spoke of therapeutic law and therapeutic legal rules. I suggested that therapeutic law is characterised by open-ended clauses, permitting open-ended applications which encourage officials such as psychiatrists to engage in ad hoc balancing of interests that resist reduction to general rules (p. 193). I saw it as being characterised by rules formulated in such a way as to permit the widest possible discretion: not only are the rules loosely formulated, they have no secondary rules which demand formal presentation of evidence, nor permit cross-examination of witnesses. Alongside this is an absence of legal safeguards; the patient is not cautioned prior to the psychiatric interview, and the psychiatrist (and others) can make the decision away from public scrutiny.

I suggested that therapeutic law differs from formal law in that formal law is concerned with rules and procedures with commands backed by threats of force to obey those rules. Classical jurisprudence saw formal law as commands issued by the sovereign and backed by sanctions, where the rules are laid down by a supreme political authority. Therapeutic law is different: it too has rules laid down by a supreme political authority but it is purposive: by that I mean the decision to apply the rules depends on a judgement about how best to achieve a purpose – in this case the best treatment for the patient. It allows choices to be made between competing values (to treat or not to treat). Formal law presents no such choices. Formal law links a specific act or omission (the crime) to a specific type of reaction (the punishment). The aim is to achieve justice which occurs when the link is made to earlier links (that is, by precedents or by comparisons with similar acts and reactions). In Aubert's terms:

> Equality before medicine is not the same type of ideal as equality before the law. To put it crudely each sick person is of supreme importance. Comparisons are out of place in a way. (quoted in Bean 1980, p. 49)

To the psychiatrist, decisions about what happens to others similarly placed are irrelevant. Psychiatric decisions are not concerned with promoting justice, nor are they based on the actions of the patient, except in as far as those actions provide information on the nature of treatment to be provided. 'Equality before medicine' concerns the outcome of the disease condition; it does not include equality of treatments. Two patients may have the same condition but require different types of treatment over different periods of time. 'Equality before the law' is different; it involves comparability and commensurability, where comparability means receiving the same punishment as others who have committed a like offence, and commensurability means being punished for having committed the offence. In Aristotelian terms, justice is achieved where equals are dealt with equally, and unequals unequally, and where the framework of relevance is about their actions, or what they have done, not on what they are.

The different epistemological traditions of psychiatry and law provoke tensions. They also help to explain some of the apparently incomprehensible features of mental health legislation, such as being deliberately vague, with poorly defined subcategories of mental disorder, where mental illness is not defined, and an absence of judicial intervention when patients are illegally detained against the rules. Where such detention occurs, the so-called 'paperwork' can be changed to fit the rules or a new assessment made by another psychiatrist. Unlike the policeman who gets things wrong, there is no public denunciation for the psychiatrist or social worker, no criminal offence has been committed and no immediate freedom for the patient to leave hospital.

Attempts to introduce measures akin to formal law have been resisted by governments and professionals alike. In the discussions preceding the 1983 Act, MIND suggested that compulsory admissions be based on behavioural criteria alone (that is, to produce evidence about past behaviour that the patient had been dangerous to self or others). In the Review of the 1959 Act, the Department of Health and the Home Office (1978, para. 1.17) said there was:

little support for this proposal. Nor has there been much evidence that the present lack of definition [of mental illness] leads to any particular problems: the government therefore proposes to leave it undefined.

A tighter definition would, it was said, restrict the clinicians ability to make choices.

Nigel Eastman and Jill Peay (1999) look at those areas where mental health law has features which distinguish it from formal law. One feature has been noted earlier, namely that mental health law does not apply, nor need apply, to all patients with similar mental health problems. It applies only to those selected by clinicians; there is no 'mental health police force' demanding that *all* who need treatment must be detained. Nor does the law insist that all who play a part in the commitment procedure be required to do so; doctors, Approved Social Workers and relatives can opt out with no acrimony attached to their actions. It is all a matter of being willing to be involved. In practice, Eastman and Peay say most professionals regard the 'law on mental health as to be avoided, for it is rarely perceived as a proper effective instrument for achieving objectives' (ibid. p. 13).

Mental health law allows the clinician to decide who should be admitted to hospital, for how long, for what reason and according to his individual diagnosis. This occurs, according to Eastman and Peay, on what they call 'a definitional morass' (ibid. p. 5), that is to say, on key terms such as 'mental disorder' or 'mental illness', with a catch-all phrase added for good measure, that of, 'any other disorder of mind'. Recently, there has been increasing scholarly interest in what is called 'therapeutic jurisprudence' (Wexler and Winnick 1996). It is a term I have some difficulty with, as, in my view, it puts the emphasis in the wrong place and puts things the wrong way round. The study is or should be about jurisprudential questions raised by therapeutic law; 'therapeutic' being the adjective referring to law and not to jurisprudence. I am also concerned about the aims of therapeutic jurisprudence, which are to uncover the therapeutic tensions in the law and encourage therapeutic outcomes. If those tensions lie within the patients, then of course they need to be identified, but if they lie within the psychiatrists, social workers and so on, then I remain to be convinced that they are important. There are always tensions among law enforcers; this is their burden. American Drug Courts, which directly involve the judge in the rehabilitation process, are another favoured area of interest (see Bean 1996).

However, things may be changing. Grisso and Applebaum (1998) have challenged some cherished assumptions about mental disorder, raising questions about the extent of legal incompetence in impaired mental states. They say:

> Until quite recently, it was common for clinicians to presume that serious mental illness, mental retardation or cognitive impairment *per se* rendered a patient incompetent to consent to treatment. This

presumption frequently was recognised in the legal system as well. Courts often accepted a clinician's diagnosis of mental illness as all that was required to settle the matter. The most fundamental, important and uncontroversial maxim we can offer about the modern concept of legal incompetence is that this presumption is obsolete. (p. 18)

There is a longstanding tendency to assert and assume that mental illness and cognitive disorders are synonymous. Patients who are psychotic, mentally retarded or demented have been considered incompetent, and, once considered, the matter was not raised again – at least until the patient was discharged from treatment. Grisso and Applebaum found that most patients hospitalised with mental illness performed certain tasks as well as a comparison group of research subjects with no history of mental disorder. With patients recently hospitalised for schizophrenia, about half of them performed as well as the non-ill comparison group (ibid. p. 19).

This research illustrates the dangers of using open-ended legal definitions which allow clinicians to make decisions unchallenged. The patient is left without rights, except the right to be given treatment. If Grisso and Applebaum are correct, then for years patients have been denied the right to make decisions and have been given treatment without consent. There have been no challenges to the clinicians' decisions – how could there be and on what grounds? The clinician has remained supreme. Georg Hoyer says 'the commitment of non dangerous patients is only justifiable when the mental capacity of the patient is reduced as a consequence of mental disorder or disability' (1999, p. 3). Were that to be accepted, it would place new restrictions on clinical freedom.

Georg Hoyer (1999) also notes that wherever countries have a mental health law, they also authorise coercion and do so in roughly the same form as in Britain. The question to be asked then is not how do we change mental health legislation from therapeutic to formal law, but how do we limit the discretion in therapeutic law to provide the necessary protection for patients? One solution offered here is to make the rules less open-ended; that at least offers a respectable form of control. Others will be offered in Chapters 2 and 3.

Conclusion

Mental health legislation raises complex questions covering numerous disciplines. Future mental health legislation may become unrecognisable from that currently in existence, dealing with matters which are now infrequently considered. Substitute decision making – used when patients lose the capacity to make treatment decisions – may well assume an increasing level of importance, with all the complexities that involves (see Grisso and Applebaum 1998, Chapter 8).

Even if new questions are asked, old ones will and should continue to appear. Questions about the justification for compulsion must always be asked. Individual autonomy has to be preserved, and, unless awkward questions are asked, professionals will proceed as if the matter was settled. Complacency surrounding the 1983 Act was astonishing (Bean 1980). Moreover, few questions have been asked about the justification for compulsion for the 1983 Act. This has allowed a paternalism to develop based on what Georg Hoyer (1999) calls the 'Thank you theory of psychiatry'. That means patients will be grateful they were compulsorily admitted, which can also be interpreted as no harm done. Never mind the loss of self-respect, the deprivation of liberty, stigma or loss of control; the 'thank you theory' shows how people are grateful, thanking all concerned that the decision was made for them (ibid. p. 9). And of course many patients are grateful. Many are grateful they were coerced, for without coercion they would never have made the decision to seek treatment. That is one of the essential dilemmas.

2

Justification for Compulsory Detention

Although most patients are dealt with informally, a small number are not. The current legislation is the 1983 Mental Health Act, where under Sections 2, 3 and 4 patients may be compulsorily admitted to a mental hospital. The Mental Health (Patients in the Community) Act 1995 (referred to hereafter as the 1995 Act) allows patients to be placed under supervision while in the community. Compulsory powers exist elsewhere, for example under the National Assistance Act 1948, where persons suffering from grave chronic disease, or being aged, or physically incapacitated and living in unsanitary conditions can be removed from home. It is to patients under the 1983 Act, however, that this chapter is dedicated.

Briefly, the 1983 Act distinguishes between admissions for assessment and admission for treatment – we are dealing here with non-offender patients. Admission for assessment can be found under Sections 2, 4, 135 and 136; admissions for treatment are under Section 3; and Guardianship under Section 7 – a provision rarely used nowadays although it is increasing. For admission for assessment the patient can be diagnosed as suffering from mental disorder – the generic term – but for admission for treatment the diagnosis must be more specific and include one of the four forms of mental disorder: mental illness, psychopathy, mental impairment or severe mental impairment. To complicate matters further, to be admitted for treatment the law distinguishes between the major disorders of mental illness and severe mental impairment, and the minor disorders of psychopathy or mental impairment. The former allows admissions to hospital even if hospital treatment is unlikely to do the patient any good, and the latter if treatment is likely to make the patient better, or at least prevent him from getting worse (Hoggett 1984, p. 42).

Similar provisions exist for mentally disordered offenders: that is, a court can make a Hospital Order or Guardianship Order under

Section 37, an interim Hospital Order under Section 38, and a Transfer Order during sentence. Under Section 47, the offender must have one of the specified forms of mental disorder. Hospital Orders during sentence also distinguish between the major and minor forms of disorder. However, the court cannot make Transfer Orders post-sentence as these are the Home Secretary's responsibility.

It is not the aim of this chapter to examine compulsion in terms of the specific legal details surrounding the various sections of the Act, for this has been done elsewhere (see Hoggett 1984 where this is done particularly well). It is worth noting, however, that these distinctions have themselves formed part of the justification for the detention of compulsory patients. The influential Percy Commission (1957), which led to the 1959 Mental Health Act, distinguished four categories of mental disorder and linked them to its justification for detention. The minor disorders (psychopathy and mental impairment – the latter term not used by the Percy Commission, this being the modern version) had limited powers associated with these conditions and were, according to the Percy Commission, sufficient to provide protection of the patients and secure their rights. This method, the Commission suggested, helped keep compulsion to a minimum. The major disorders, mental illness and severe mental impairment, required more powers and, accordingly, more compulsion was thought likely to be required.

These distinctions, although important, do not provide the major focus of this discussion. The aim here is to seek justification in socio-legal terms for detaining non-offender patients against their will. All countries accept the need for compulsory commitment, although the methods and justification may vary, but no country has rejected civil commitment, although some countries have no specific legislation per se. In Britain, many of the origins of civil commitment can be found in the Poor Law, or in common law.

Compulsory admissions: an assessment

The most important feature in the last 30 years or so relating to mental health policy has been the decarceration movement, which removed virtually all the old-style mental hospitals from the face of Britain. A small number remain, but new, smaller, purpose-built accommodation has replaced them. For example, Nottinghamshire once had two mental hospitals, at their peak holding together over 2,000 patients. These have been replaced by smaller units, some purpose built, so that now only about 200 hospital beds are available and these mainly for acute patients. The chronic tend to be treated in general hospitals where there is a shortage of beds for these patients.

Such changes are without parallel in the history of mental health policy. They have revolutionised thinking, raising new questions about how best to deal with patients, whether in the hospital or the community. They require health service personnel to meet new challenges to working practices. Old certainties have disappeared, where the physical and legal controls provided in the mental hospitals have been replaced by mental health teams operating in the community. While many thousands of patients have been discharged from hospitals, it is often forgotten that psychiatrists and others have also been decarcerated, requiring them to adjust to these new ways. The changes have not always been easy. One obvious challenge has been to adjust to a reduction in acute and chronic beds, and to a shorter length of stay, now about three weeks – in the 1970s it was about three months.

It is reasonable to assume that there has been a reduction in the numbers and proportion of patients commited to hospital. I say reasonable to assume because no one knows the exact figures. The data on which these assumptions are based remain at best uneven and at worst poor. To digress for a moment: data are produced annually by the Department of Health in their Statistical Bulletin. In a research study concerned with assessing the extent of compulsory admissions in the London area, these data were found to bear little resemblance to the data produced by the hospitals, or in the official statistics. Some examples are given in Tables 2.1 and 2.2: data were taken from three hospitals in the South West Thames Regional Health Authority for the year 1989–90. The Fylde and district data are as the official statistics (Nemitz and Bean 1995). The range of differences were not always as wide as this, yet of the 23 hospitals under examination, 10 of them had differences greater than 30%, and in only one hospital was there agreement.

On the basis of these results, and assuming these hospitals were representative of those throughout England and Wales, it is difficult to see how the official data are of much value, whether for planning or research. Hospitals with apparently low admission rates turned out, on closer inspection, to have rather more, and those with higher admission rates turned out to have rather fewer. What effect do these inadequate data have on the work of those planning services, or on the Mental Health Act Commission? Which set of data is to be given to the commissioners on their visits, and how can they protect patient's rights without knowing how many patients are detained? And what is the financial cost of producing such data with so little value? The solution proposed in our research (ibid. p. 32) was that all compulsory admissions be notified

Table 2.1 Returns from 1 April 1989 to 31 March 1990

	Unit level	District level	Fylde data
Hospital A			
Section 2	41	41	41
Section 3	16	12	12
Section 4	4	4	4
Hospital B			
Section 2	44	60	60
Section 3	17	22	22
Section 4	8	15	15

Table 2.2 Returns from 1 April 1989 to 31 March 1990

	Unit level	District level	Fylde data
Hospital C			
Section 2	213	137	137
Section 3	123	42	42
Section 4	51	78	78
Hospital D			
Section 2	40	82	82
Section 3	13	20	20
Section 4	53	108	108

direct to the Mental Health Act Commission (as in Scotland) where the Commission would collect, analyse and publish the data in a more appropriate form. Errors could be reduced as well as cost.

To return to the main argument: community care gathered pace throughout the late 1980s and early 1990s. Initially strongly supported by the then government, it was not without its critics. Some saw it as failing to provide adequate services, others, including the more vocal focus groups, as failing to provide adequate protection to members of the community. These critics have had an important impact on government policy, being largely responsible for promoting demands for more community safety and changing perceptions of the mentally disordered.

In July 1998, the Health Secretary called for a new approach to mental health care and confirmed that there was no possibility of a return to the old-style mental hospitals, which, he said, involved 'locking up mentally ill patients in long stay institutions so they are out of sight and out of mind' (Department of Health press release 1998a). Nor did it involve moving to an accelerated community care programme. Rather the aim was to set more optimistic standards for mental health. It would produce 'a system in which both patients and public are safe and sound – a system which provides both security and support to all who need it' (ibid. 1998a).

Here was a change in emphasis. In the 1960s and 70s the government's aims were to provide appropriate services for treating the mentally disordered – this being the basic premise on which the legislation was based. The emphasis then was on the patient's right to treatment. By the 1980s that had finally shifted to a greater concern for government spending, hence the move to decarceration and community care, a move which began earlier but reached its peak in the 1980s. The emphasis shifted again in the 1990s to one of community safety, with special concern for those who are 'a danger to themselves and a nuisance to others'.

Paul Boateng, the then Parliamentary Under Secretary of State for Health, thought public confidence had been affected by reports of enquiries into a number of tragic incidents which pointed to gaps in service provision. These included failure to act by the medical services themselves, failure to provide information for other agencies and failures to diagnose psychotic conditions and identify dangerous patients (Department of Health press release 1998b). He said the new approach would be expected to provide prompt, responsive and efficient access to health and social care, followed where necessary by admissions to an acute hospital bed. This would be backed by other treatments given in a range of settings, secure or otherwise, depending on what was deemed appropriate. They would include an 'assertive outreach' strategy directed 'at those who are in danger of falling through the net' and 'to inner cities whose rates of severe mental illness are higher and people harder to reach because of higher levels of homelessness and social isolation' (ibid. 1998b). Such patients will be required to receive treatment against their wishes if necessary and in secure institutions if required. Community safety had arrived and become the watchword.

In some respects of course any new legislation will operate much as before. However, The Department of Health talk of a 'New vision for mental health services', presumably aiming to break away from the traditional approach towards a new philosophy of care. How far that can be achieved and be successful remains to be seen. The 'new vision' of mental health services proposed by the Department of Health has three principal aims. They are:

1   to protect the public and provide effective and safe care for those
    with severe and enduring mental illness

2   to meet the needs of those with mental health problems who can appropriately and safely be managed within primary health and social care
3   to promote good mental health in the population and help build healthier neighbourhoods.

The essential components are:

1   access: prompt, responsive and efficient access to health and social care
2   treatment and care: ensuring there are enough beds of the right sort and in the right places
3   continuing care, rehabilitation and support services: those who are not recovering will need continuing support and help from services sometimes for the rest of their lives (ibid. 1998b)

The government believes that new legislation is required, although in my opinion the evidence for that change has not been produced, by government or elsewhere. With one or two exceptions, the 1983 Act works pretty well. Frank Dobson again:

The law on mental health is based on the needs and therapies of a bygone age. Its revision in 1983 merely tinkered with the problem. What I want now is a root and branch review to reflect the opportunities and limits of modern therapies and drugs. (written answer to a parliamentary question August 1998)

If there really is to be a 'root and branch review', this is to be welcomed. And if so, two basic questions are to be answered; first, what is the aim and purpose of mental health law, and second, how can provisions for non-offender patients be justified? Neither question is easy, but looking through the Department of Health proposals one suspects that the answers may have already been given. The Health Secretary said in August 1998:

It [the new legislation] will cover such possible measures as compliance orders and community treatment orders to provide a prompt and effective legal basis to ensure that patients get supervised care if they do not take their medication or if their condition deteriorates. (ibid.)

No hint here of any agonising over philosophical and jurisprudential questions concerning compulsion, and no hint later in the Report of the

Expert Committee (Department of Health 1999), in their *Review of the Mental Health Act 1983*, who discuss and seem to dismiss the problem too easily. Rather, there is a self-evident justification that compulsion is required, where things will continue much as before, or if anything be extended. It is assumed that there is no need to debate the question further (ibid. 1999). (Some justification, however, can be found on the Department of Health website, Bean, P.T., *Justifying Compulsion*.)

Assuming, however, that the government is serious and wants a 'root and branch' review, what then? Will there really be a radical departure, or will the end result be pretty much as before? The answer is probably, as before. In saying this I am not being overcritical of the government, for it is rarely possible to break with the past, sometimes tinkering is all that one can do. The law is a pragmatic instrument, working with what is available, and constantly drawing on existing practices. In Britain that means providing the usual mixture of care and control in settings that are well established. We can tinker with some bits of legislation but that is all. The 1983 Act did some useful tinkering; it softened the therapeutic excesses of the 1959 Act where the right to treatment was supreme, and introduced *inter alia* consent to treatment provisions which were path breaking. But it left alone the central features of compulsory powers, and retained the same structure as the 1890 Lunacy Act. New legislation will almost certainly do likewise, retaining structures which have worked well in the past and with which users are familiar. The decision is about which bits to tinker with, and which new features to introduce. The fear is that there will be tinkering with the important bits and massive changes made to the unimportant.

What is the aim and purpose of mental health law?

To the main question, what is the aim and purpose of mental health law, there are subsidiary questions, such as what can the law do? Or what will changing the rules achieve, and what is the likely outcome of those changes on psychiatric practices? There is no point requiring patients to be dealt with in such and such a way if appropriate services do not exist, or existing practices are unable to change sufficiently to accommodate them. Underpinning all these questions is that which seeks a justification for laws involving compulsory detention – one of the great unanswered and timeless questions of all.

Larry Gostin (1983) set out three broad aims for mental health law; first, to give the patients a right to adequate health and social services, second, to set limits on psychiatric activities based upon the principles of consent, and finally, to prevent discrimination on the basis of a psychiatric classification. Gostin saw the law as but one of a number of strategies for securing a comprehensive mental health system (p. 27). There are others, but Gostin's model can be used to determine a justification for compulsion, which, incidentally, he did not try to do, although much of what he said implied that these were his aims.

The right to adequate health and social services

Gostin argued that patients had what he called an 'ideology of entitlement'. By this he meant that access to health and social services should not be based upon charitable or professional discretion but upon enforceable rights. That is to say, Parliament is not obliged to pass legislation to provide those services, but should it do so it cannot arbitrarily deprive or exclude individuals or client groups (ibid. p. 30). The role of law is to establish the right to services, which can be enforced at the behest of any client group or individual (ibid. p. 30).

Gostin recognised that this approach relies on what he calls open-textured or enabling legislation; that is, legislation which is supported by adequate financing, efficient management, and good practice, otherwise services would be inadequate. So for example, services may meet strict legal criteria but fail in other respects: they could be set in the wrong place, be poorly delivered, or fail to reach the target population. Gostin saw the right to services as a proper duty of law. The law, he says, provides rules from which rights are derived, at the same time giving duties to others, in this case local authorities or government departments. This applies whether these services are for the prevention, diagnosis or treatment of mental disorder. Among the many reasons Gostin gave to support the ideology of entitlement is that it becomes a means of drawing attention to and making comparisons with other measures to secure a fair proportion of resources within the mental health system. Mental health services have traditionally been the poor relation of medicine, acquiring a smaller proportion of the total budget. The ideology of entitlement readdresses that balance.

Gostin is correct at one level, but matters are more complicated than this (Bean 1986, p. 80). In legal terms, rights must be secured by a remedy if they are violated, and the law should protect those rights. That much is clear. But what the ideology of entitlement cannot do is determine the quality of the services, or determine to whom they should be given. These are not matters of law but of professional judgement, where professionals decide according to their professional considerations. The professional is a gatekeeper, deciding who to accept or exclude; decisions are based on professional demands and interests. For example, mentally disordered patients who are also substance abusers with high rates of medical non-compliance and producing high levels of disruption may be and often are denied appropriate services. Or psychiatrists in regional secure units invariably develop policies deciding who shall be admitted – and incidentally have traditionally excluded patients from special hospitals awaiting transfer. Or again, social work professionals can and often do decide who are to be recipients of their services, for example, white prospective adopters have been denied the opportunity to adopt black or mixed race children (ibid. 1986).

Gostin is not wrong to believe that the law has a place in securing services for the mentally disordered but he needs to do rather more than assume that the legal requirements to provide services will directly affect the quality of these services. Quality is determined as much by professional interpretations of these services as by the legal demand to introduce them. To paraphrase Brenda Hoggett (1984), we should not expect much from the courts when it comes to enforcing these types of rights, for English law cuts a pretty poor figure in this area, preferring to leave any entitlement to those operating the services. At best the ideology of entitlement acts as a way of drawing attention to the under-provision of services, and to any underresourcing that may occur.

That apart, is the ideology of entitlement an appropriate area for mental health law? Historically speaking, perhaps not. The 1890 Lunacy Act did not concern itself with the provision of services, but with regulating the professionals operating those services. Similarly, the 1959 Mental Health Act left decisions to the professionals to determine how treatment be provided. The 1983 Mental Health Act amended those provisions but added little to them. Recent legislation involving supervision in the community under the Mental Health (Patients in the Community) Act 1995 was more concerned with providing criteria to minimise inappropriate use, and to be non-discriminatory in principle and practice, than with the provisions of the services themselves, although to some extent it required local authorities to provide certain additional services. Setting out the framework is it seems as far as Parliament has been prepared to go.

Some political theorists think Parliament is wise to go no further. Law, they say, is a function of the political economy of the state and is as much about limiting access to services as providing an entitlement to them. Access can be limited in a number of ways, one of which is to change the criteria for compulsory admissions. For example, the Under Secretary of State for Health has a vision of the type of services to be provided and these include, 'a commitment to the historic principle of a national health service designed to provide treatment and care, delivered on the basis of need rather than income, occupation, level of education, origin, gender or age' (Department of Health press release 1998b).

This vision is presented in such a high order of generality, and without specific reference to this or that service that it becomes virtually impossible to call into account any failure by the state to provide a service, let alone reach a level of service provision. What it does is arouse expectations and suggest entitlements, but does so in such a way as to avoid accusations of failure when they are not met thereafter.

Another ruse is to draft legislation in such a way as to restrict the use of those services – not in the sense of simply excluding patients by decree, but by more subtle means, such as using moral or civil rights arguments to promote an ideology which has its own limiting effect. For example, once a patient has been compulsorily admitted to hospital, the state has an obligation to provide treatment; there being no other reason to detain him there. What better way to restrict the demands of treatment than to redraft the legislation to make it more difficult to admit – adding, perhaps, doubts about the nature and existence of mental illness or questioning the efficacy and value of psychiatric treatment. These tactics were used in North America to restrict state spending. They distort the debate about compulsory admissions and undermine the accepted concern for rights, treatment and liberties, and show how mental health legislation can become an ideological and political tool. The way to counter this is to make it clear that *all* patients, compulsory or otherwise, must receive the same quality of care.

Emphasising the right to adequate health care and services has the obvious and intended effect of shifting the emphasis from the behaviour of the sick person to the available services. That is to say, the debate places the onus on the service providers, not on the service users, and inturn promotes a welcome change of direction; it attempts to create a legal framework to provide choices for those whether in hospital or the community (Bingley 1985, p. 202). It also tries to hold politicians accountable. Even so, defects and loopholes will remain and are to be expected; no mental health legislation is ever free from them.

Limits of psychiatric services based in part on the principle of consent

Gostin's second strategy is 'to set limits on psychiatric activities based in part upon the principles of consent'. That means that the expert must explain and justify his decision to detain patients against their will, according to some objective criteria. Experts must give the grounds for their decision in terms that are open to examination. Gostin insists that this is not a proposition derived from any anti-psychiatry movement, but from an appropriate legal approach which cannot accept unsupported claims to knowledge in areas of diagnosis, behaviour prediction, or treatment (Gostin 1983, p. 38).

Setting limits on psychiatric activities lies at the heart of the matter, and that includes civil commitment – whether to hospital, or for supervision of patients in the community – and consent to treatment, where consent overrides the powers to treat under compulsion. That is to say, it determines when compulsion should cease – for offender patients that could include the decisions of Mental Health Review Tribunals, and for non-offender patients includes being discharged from hospital. However, defining what is meant by being discharged from hospital is more complicated than it seems. Once, discharge meant simply leaving the hospital, the decision being made by the psychiatrist on clinical and social grounds that the patient's condition was in remission. Nowadays nearly everyone leaves whether they are ready or not, even if they are not able to survive in the community. Bean and Mounser (1993, pp. 11–16) thought a more appropriate definition of a discharge was 'ceasing to have contact with the mental health team, whether in the hospital or community'. This is, of course, an altogether different matter. What it does not do is provide a general justification for compulsory detention, for it concentrates on what happens to patients when they are detained. That justification is now required.

Justifying compulsory detention

We can begin by asserting an obvious yet necessary moral position; it has long been a tradition of English law that justifications are required when freedoms are taken away and rights similarly removed. Compulsory admission to a mental hospital, and compulsory supervision in the community, involves a loss of freedom. That a person can be put under restraint and taken to a place where he can be detained and given treatment without consent is, according to the tradition of English law, a matter that requires justification. That the restraint occurs without due process of law, as signified by the order of a judicial officer and without a right of appeal prior to committal, further compounds the process.

The law concerning compulsory admissions to mental hospitals has been a central feature of all current, and earlier, Mental Health Acts over the past 150 years (for the present, the use of community powers will be left aside); so much so that we may easily take it for granted that mentally disordered people might wish to be detained and receive treatment. Moreover, powers for compulsory admission are now so much part of mental health legislation that we may begin to accept them uncritically, or we may regard them as necessary and operating in the patients' best interests; supported perhaps by the belief that patients will recognise eventually that they were ill and approve when their treatment is completed – the so-called 'thank you' model of psychiatry. We may believe there is no credible alternative, in which case there is no need to justify the loss of freedom and the ensuing loss of rights that compulsory admissions involve. That would be a dangerous position to get into. On what basis, then, can compulsory powers be justified?

Traditionally, solutions have been sought by tying the debate into socio-political arguments. The Percy Commission (1957), and the Macmillan Commission (1926) that preceded it, asserted that 'mental illness is an illness like any other illness', even though the basis of their case was far from secure. They did so because they wished to promote psychiatry to the rank of a discipline equal to, and able to run alongside, other medical specialisms. Conversely, the anti-psychiatry movement has disputed the right of psychiatry to deal with those mental disorders defined and covered by existing legislation, preferring to talk of 'a problem of living', and seeing no justification whatsoever for compulsory detention. And so the battle lines are drawn.

Complications have arisen, and still arise, because of the absence of research concerning the way the Act operates. This is not just a British problem, it occurs elsewhere, in Canada for example (Verdon-Jones, personal communication), yet astonishingly in Britain, research into the use of compulsory powers, which after all involve a major form of restraint, has been almost totally neglected. Rarely have we asked whether the use of these powers was effective, necessary or whether they assisted treatment.

Nor have there been many debates on the boundaries of the subject matter. Some somatic conditions produce disorders similar to those found in conventional psychiatry, but are not included in the legislation, except perhaps the toxic confusional states. Why not? Or rather should they be? These questions may appear to go beyond the debate on compulsion, but in fact are highly relevant, for we are entitled to know the conditions which psychiatry seeks to treat and which lie outside its provenance.

Compulsory powers have been justified in the following ways. First, on the basis that some form of mental disorder be present 'of a nature or degree that warrants compulsion', where the patient's condition can be determined clinically according to current diagnostic knowledge and the service facilities available. Second, justifications have been made on the basis of what I have called 'other conditions' of which three are identified. First, that which comes under the general heading of *parens patriae*, second, that defined by the Percy Commission which we can call the right to treatment, and finally on the basis of public safety. These so-called 'other conditions' are not discrete, there is much over-lap. Nor, to complicate matters, do they cover the entire debate, and they have often been called on to provide a justification in their own right. However, it is probable that these 'other conditions' have been presented as a composite package. So, for example, supporters of the right to treatment have never claimed that it was a sufficient justifi-cation of itself to detain a person in a mental hospital, there had to be a danger to the patient and/or to others as well. Similarly, those justifying compulsion on *parens patriae* grounds have never wanted to claim that this was sufficient of itself, and have included other criteria, such as levels of dangerousness.

These 'other conditions' will be examined separately. Yet, if only to repeat the point, the tendency has been to mix them, and produce an end product made to appear as if it was a coherent whole. For example, the Percy Commission justified compulsion on the grounds of the right to treatment, then added a secondary justification – *parens patriae* – followed by a third, that of community safety; a pattern, incidentally, found in earlier Royal Commissions. The Report of the Expert Com-mittee (Department of Health 1999) mixed two main justifications in their overview of compulsory powers, stating that the 'primary purpose of mental health legislation is to provide a framework for the appro-priate exercise of compulsory powers'. The Expert Committee then justified compulsory powers on much the same basis as the Percy Com-mission, adding an element of *parens patriae*, but not, strangely enough, seeming to be concerned with personal safety, to self or others. The Expert Committee (ibid. 1999) put it this way:

> where a patient lacks the capacity to consent to care and treatment for mental disorder then society should have the power to provide that care and treatment even in the absence of that person's consent. Thus the primary function... is to enable mental health services to care appropriately for those who are unable to authorise that care and treatment themselves.

It is odd, and rather disturbing, that this is the only justification provided in what was to be 'a root and branch' review of legislation. If evidence were required about the lack of concern to justify compulsory admissions, this is it.

Parens patriae

While there has long been a tradition in English law that a loss of freedom requires justification, so too has there been a tradition that intervention can be justified, if the aim is to protect the person from his inability to care for himself. This proposition occurs under the ancient concept of *parens patriae*, that is literally the state as father of the people, where it is the duty of the state to look after those who are unable to look after themselves. An early manifestation of *parens patriae* in English law was the recognition by Edward the Second in the 14th century of the sovereign's responsibility towards the property, and later the person, of the insane (Kittrie 1971, p. 9). A modern example, albeit in a slightly different context, can be found under the National Assistance Act 1948, whereby some elderly people can be removed from their home when they cannot care for themselves.

Another modern example of the use of *parens patriae* can be found in the Percy Commission Report (1957, para. 211), where it quotes from an earlier Royal Commission on the Care of the Feeble Minded written at the beginning of this century:

> Our first principle is that persons who cannot take a part in the struggle of life owing to mental defect... should be afforded by the State such general protection as may be suited to their needs. Heretofore, lunatics, idiots, and imbeciles have received the protection of the Law. We propose that this principle of special protection should be extended to all mentally defective persons.
>
> These and other advantages we hope may follow... from the certification and provisions which depend on it.

Under *parens patriae* certification is a privilege which brings benefits. As the state has a duty of care so its agents have a duty to see that care is offered in the circumstances appropriate to the person's needs. In its purist form there is no interest in the aetiology of the condition; its effects are the important determinants. To qualify for *parens patriae* those effects must leave the patient incapable of caring for himself.

In one sense, of course, aetiology is important, for the case for *parens patriae* is better made if the patient's condition is seen as a result of a lack of responsibility to make other than harmful decisions. There are numerous historical precedents for this; Kittrie describes how the insane of the 17th and 18th centuries lacked responsibility, and how in the history of unreason the insane were gradually segregated from the criminals. Madness itself became a problem in its own right (Kittrie 1971, p. 61). In its extreme forms, and when it can be shown that there is a defect of reason occurring as a result of mental disorder, the person can be exonerated from any criminal act. In less dramatic, more routine occurrences, it is enough to assert that the person has lost some power of reasoning and is not fully responsible for his actions: the court may then accept this as mitigation.

On a technical point, the case for *parens patriae* is strengthened if it can be shown that the mental condition, in whatever form it arose, did not arise by choice; that is to say, it was something that happened to the person, and not something done deliberately. The anti-psychiatrists' case is that 'the something', which psychiatrists call mental illness, is not a happening at all but behaviour which arises from choice, in which case it becomes mere dislike. They add that behaviour which involves harm to others is a matter for the criminal law, while self-harm is not the law's business. But whether one is an anti-psychiatry supporter or not, if that 'happening' occurred irrespective of the person's wishes – and it is up to those supporting compulsion in whatever form to say it did – no blame can be attributed. If it did not, then the person is blameworthy and responsible for his actions.

Parens patriae is rarely used nowadays as a justification for detaining the insane, or for the intervention of compulsory supervision. Its peak in popularity was in the 1970s when the welfare state was in its heyday, indeed some commentators see the growth of the welfare state as nothing more than an extension of *parens patriae* powers. By the 1990s, *parens patriae* became a perjorative term, being too closely associated with a wider critique of the so-called therapeutic state. It still remains a potent force where intervention can be justified on *parens patriae* grounds so that:

> For the elderly patient suffering from senile dementia, the mentally retarded, the neglected child, and the skid row alcoholic, the therapeutic state is not as much an instrument for reformation as a public welfare service. (Kittrie 1971, p. 385)

Critics of *parens patriae* see it as providing an excuse for imposing an increasing number of social controls – the modern term is 'net

widening' – and for imposing greater measures of preventative detention under the guise of providing help.

> As long as therapeutic science and skills remain underdeveloped,
> confinement in the name of *parens patriae* was almost certainly more
> of a preventative detention measure for the benefit of society than an
> individually orientated programme. (ibid. p. 61)

While *parens patriae* is no longer the force it once was, and few would
cite it nowadays as a justification for compulsory detention, it is occasionally smuggled in to justify intervention to improve patient care.
Nowadays, *parens patriae* is associated with paternalism, but its strength
is to awaken us to the needs of the less fortunate. Its weakness is to
permit intrusion into people's lives, based on the judgements of those
claiming to know best. In mental health terms, that means giving treatment against the patients' wishes.

Treatment

Those wanting to justify compulsory powers on the basis of treatment
will find the most eloquent case in the Report of the Percy Commission
(1957). The Commission said the use of compulsory powers was justified when the mental disorder was seen to distort perception in such
a way as to affect the person's ability to care for himself. That is to say
when:

(a) there is reasonable certainty that the patient is suffering from a
     pathological mental disorder and requires hospital or community
     care; and,
(b) suitable care cannot be provided without the use of compulsory
     powers; and,
(c) if the patient himself is unwilling to receive the form of care which
     is considered necessary, there is at least a strong likelihood that his
     unwillingness is due to a lack of appreciation of his own condition
     deriving from the mental disorder itself; and
(d) there is also either,

  (i) good prospect of benefit to the patient from the treatment
       proposed – an expectation that it will either cure or alleviate
       his mental disorder or strengthen his ability to regulate his
       social behaviour in spite of the underlying disorder, or bring

him substantial benefit in the form of protection from neglect
or exploitation by others; or,

(ii)   a strong need to protect others from anti-social behaviour by
the patient. (para. 317)

In the preceding paragraph of the Report, the Percy Commission add a
further justification:

No one disputes that there are some circumstances in which society
must in the last resort be able to compel some patients to receive
treatment or training in their own interests or for the protection of
others, and that some may need to be protected against exploitation
or neglect. (para. 316)

The main principles of the Percy Commission were accepted by the
then government and translated and incorporated into the 1959 Mental
Health Act, albeit with some modifications. The 1983 Mental Health
Act retained much of that earlier legislation, making other minor
changes – mainly amending the statutes – but without challenging the
Percy Commission's arguments. In essence, then, current legislation
remains centred on the Percy Commission's formulations, retaining its
basic assumptions.

The great strength of the Percy Commission's position is that it
stressed the value of competency by promoting a model of psychiatry
derived from medicine. That model is capable of extending, yet also
limiting, the scope of psychiatric intervention and competence, which
from the legal point of view is entirely satisfactory (Hoggett 1984,
p. 39). It lays no claim to solving all the ills that the flesh is heir to (ibid.
p. 39). It encourages a scientific approach to the study and treatment of
mental disorder, where, through painstaking observations and experimentation, the aim is to reduce pain and alleviate distress. It does so
while still searching for the underlying defect, proceeding as if there was
an underlying disease or condition creating the signs and symptoms which
the patient and physician should describe. It emphasises the scientific
(medical) rather than the moral components of mental disorder, and,
in contrast to *parens patriae*, places the emphasis on treatment rather
than care.

There still remains the problem of compulsory powers. As we do
not compulsorily detain patients who suffer from other illnesses, why
then for mental illness or mental disorder? The Commission's reply was
to assert that, while mental illness was an illness, it nonetheless had
distinctive features. It had one special condition:

In many cases it affects the patient's judgement so that he does not realise he is ill, and the illness can only be treated against his wishes at the time. (Percy Commission, para. 314)

Eric Matthews (1999, p. 50) sees what he calls the 'baleful influence of Cartesian mind body dualism' here, where Cartesian assumptions distinguish between bodily and mental illnesses, the former being an expression of mechanical breakdown. The mind, on the other hand:

> is more than a mechanism by which we realise our conceptions and intentions: it is our self... It is *essentially* different from bodily illness, and so needs different kinds of treatment, both in the clinical and in the legal sense. (ibid. p. 50)

The Percy Commission left itself open to the obvious criticism that it was giving free rein to psychiatrists to do almost anything they wished on the grounds that they know best. Yet given its initial premise, it is difficult to know what else the Commission could say. It made the point repeatedly, without giving much evidence to support it, that admission to hospital against the patients' wishes may be the only way of providing patients with the treatment or training to restore them to health.

> When an illness or disability itself affects the patient's power of judgement and appreciative of his own condition there is a special strong argument for saying that his own interest demands that the decision whether or not to accept medical examination, care or treatment should not be left entirely to his own distorted or defective judgement. (para. 314(i))

The manner in which the Commission's arguments were translated into legislation need not concern us here. It was the emphasis on the importance of treatment given by qualified physicians which characterises the Report and this set the tone and the aspirations for at least a generation. This is all the more reason then to be clear about the disease conditions to be diagnosed and treated. What is missing from the 1959 and 1983 Acts is an adequate definition of the key terms 'mental disorder' and 'mental illness'. Open-ended definitions *inter alia* send the wrong messages, in this case doing what Brenda Hoggett describes as 'placing the psychiatrist too high and the patient too low' (op. cit. p. 67); and they raise the obvious suspicions that the patients are being misled, or misinformed, about the condition which is said to justify intervention.

If mental illness is not defined because it cannot be defined, we are entitled to wonder if the professionals themselves know what it means; and if it is not defined when it can be defined, then we are right to be suspicious about the intentions of the lawmakers. This point can be made without seeking to enter that debate about what is or what is not, say, a psychopathic disorder, or whether legal definitions of mental disorder should be on behavioural criteria alone, as suggested by MIND in the debate leading to the 1983 Act (Department of Health/ Home Office 1978). The point to be made here is more general: it is about promoting an understandable definition, which is open to examination by any competent authority; it is about clarifying what is being done. It will not do, as the Review of the 1959 Act said in 1978, that 'Nor has there been such evidence that the present lack of definition of mental illness leads to any particular problem' (ibid. para. 1.17). There may not be a problem for those who enforce the law, but there may be one for those subject to it. The law should identify and focus attention on those matters, and clarify the differences between those who are detained and the rest of us.

That aside, what of the Percy Commission's justifications? What of this so-called pathological mental disorder? Is being mentally disordered and needing treatment of itself a sufficient ground for depriving a person of his liberty? Is something else required? One approach is to do what Brenda Hoggett (1984, p. 66) suggests and start from the assumption that mental patients are people like anyone else and entitled to the same rights and then to ask which conditions entitle us to take away their rights. What is there about the mentally disordered that justifies seeing them as qualitatively different and removing their rights? The Percy Commission says the mentally disordered require treatment and hospital care, which cannot be provided elsewhere.

If this is so, the physician must find evidence of a condition which he is prepared to call a mental disorder. This point may appear obvious, but only if we accept a number of assumptions on which this statement is predicated; that evidence of a mental disorder can be produced, that the medical profession have the relevant expertise to identify those disorders, and that distinctions can be made, so that some can be classified as more serious and life threatening than others. This need not hold up the debate but it is worth noting that acceptance of a number of propositions about mental disorder which we now take for granted are of recent origin. Moreover, some commentators in the anti-psychiatry movement refuse to be convinced that the medical profession has the expertise to diagnose and treat mental disorder, not least because the term itself is misleading and a metaphor (Szasz 1983).

In 1927 the Macmillan Commission (which led to the 1930 Mental Treatment Act) sought to distinguish a mental from a physical illness. They said there was a difference in symptoms; a disease was mental if its symptoms manifest themselves predominantly in derangement of conduct, and physical if its symptoms manifest themselves predominantly in derangement of bodily functions (quoted in Bean 1980, p. 23). Such an unproblematic view would not easily be accepted nowadays.

Central to the Percy Commission's view is the assertion that if the patient is unwilling to receive treatment, that of itself demonstrates a strong likelihood that the unwillingness is due to the mental disorder (para. 317). This comes dangerously close to saying that the patient's refusal to accept help is part of the diagnosis, and equally close to saying that compulsion is necessary whenever treatment is required. There is no room here for the competent refuser, but much room for the proposition that the patient will be grateful when treatment is complete. As a matter of fact, gratitude is often expressed, but that is not sufficient of itself to warrant loss of liberty.

Community safety

Justifying compulsion on the basis of community safety is more straightforward, for it is based on the demand to protect others from the actions of the mentally disordered. Certainly, we are entitled to be protected from those who would harm us, and some mentally disordered are more than capable of inflicting harm, whether to strangers or acquaintances. Accordingly, reports on a number of fatalities by the mentally disordered (Royal College of Psychiatrists 1996) have been part of a series of pressures to introduce more effective controls.

Supporters of community safety make or assume there is a link between mental disorder and danger, emphasising the unpredictable nature of the mentally disordered. An Act of 1872 describes 'dangerous lunatics' who:

> by lunacy or otherwise are furiously mad, or are so far disordered in their senses that they may be too dangerous to be permitted to go abroad. These may be apprehended and kept safely locked in some secure place for and during such time only as such lunacy or madness shall continue. (quoted in the Percy Commission Report 1957, para. 199)

In its modern form, the supporting Supervision Registers and the Supervised Discharge Order have been the embodiment of modern community safety. The *Health Service Guidelines for the Introduction of Supervision Registers* (Department of Health 1994) require all health authorities to have 'Registers which identify and provide information on patients who are likely to be at risk of committing serious violence'. Supervised Discharge Orders are justified when 'there would be a substantial risk of serious harm to the health or safety of the patient and the safety of other people'. There is now a burgeoning community safety industry where clinicians, statisticians, psychologists and so on are busily producing risk assessments on persons likely to commit serious offences or be a threat to public safety – they were once concerned with predicting dangerousness but predicting risk is said to be easier and less contentious. They receive support from some highly vocal pressure groups that demand ever-increasing controls over the mentally disordered, and in doing so articulate public fears.

'Community safety' is fast becoming a catch-all term. The conditions for the Supervised Discharge Order include 'a substantial risk of serious harm to the safety of other people'. What are we to make of that? Is the harm to include psychological harm or just physical harm? Would it include stress? Consider the hypothetical case of a family with a hypomanic teenage son. Is the young man's family to be protected from the stress he creates? Is someone, his family perhaps, to be protected from the stress caused by his hair-brained schemes? Relatives may well need respite care to relieve stress from elderly demented relatives but to whom do they turn when the patient is young, and the consequences of his actions become apparent?

The impression created by recent legislation is that community safety is to be more narrowly defined, covering protection only from physical harm. This may be an advance over the earlier open-ended view but even so is this legislation really necessary? Supporters of community safety want to extend the level of protection to include protection from anticipated harm – that is, they want preventative detention. They do not say all mental patients are dangerous – although sometimes they come close to saying this – they say some are and they need to be identified and restrained.

Never mind for the moment the difficulties involved in predicting harm, and never mind that some patients who commit very serious harm do so in circumstances which are unpredictable – the report on Jason Mitchell said his killings were 'unpredictable and in any meaningful sense not preventable' (Blom-Cooper et al. 1996, p. 273). These are technical questions which, although important, are not directly relevant to the question examined here. The main point is that mental health law, if it takes on board the community safety programme, will include matters which the criminal law has traditionally avoided. A key principle of English law is that the law should only be invoked after a crime has been committed, and it has always been uneasy about moving from that retributive base to deal with assessments of what people are rather than what they have done. Occasionally it has wandered into the preventative realm, but when it has it invariably failed to impress.

In contrast, supporters of community safety say that preventative custody – for that is what they are talking about – saves lives and reduces harm. They point to incidents involving fatalities and claim, correctly, that some were predicted and therefore preventable. They also claim that compulsory detention may not be needed always, that community supervision may be sufficient, but compulsion in some form will be necessary. That their predictions may occasionally produce false positives (when they overpredict) and false negatives (when they underpredict) is acceptable, for they would say that such failings have to be set against the overall benefits provided to the public at large.

Yet even if this is true, to what extent should such a matter be the province of mental health legislation or, to quote Brenda Hoggett, 'should the machinery of civil commitment be used for this purpose?' (1996, p. 70). She says civil commitment has enormous advantages over the criminal process, not only for the authorities but also for others, but the risks are manifest. In effect, 'if we are creating a special sort of crime called "anti social disorder" should we not admit it?' (1984, p. 70). Perhaps we should. The procedures for civil commitment lack the restraints of the criminal law. There are no rules of evidence, no cross-examinations, no witnesses to be called, and no right of appeal prior to detention. Community safety, as defined here, operates according to the clinical decisions of the Responsible Medical Officer. Whether that clashes with Article 5(4) of the European Commission on Human Rights (ECHR) remains to be seen. (ECHR requires 'due process' in law, which means that decisions involving loss of liberty can be reviewed by a court, while rules concerning fairness and impartiality must be observed by any administrative body or tribunal.) If community safety is to be embraced further in the current form and direction, the ECHR might have important things to say.

An overview and some remaining questions

All these so-called 'other justifications' have their strengths and weaknesses, for none is able to provide a satisfactory justification in itself. Perhaps we should not be surprised, and greet that statement with some relief. In matters such as this, certainty is unwelcome, giving the impression that no further debate is required. That can and should never be so. However, a more active research programme could ease some of that uncertainty. To repeat the point; it is astonishing that so little research has been undertaken on compulsion with the obvious result that a government committee appointed in 1998 to review the 1983 Act has little data on the way the Act operates (Richardson 1999). Research will not answer the underlying philosophical questions, but it will help with questions about effectiveness, including the effectiveness of compulsion on patient outcome.

Listed below are two sets of questions which should be asked of all current legislation. Looking through the literature, it seems that sometimes we in Britain have appeared to justify compulsion according to historical precedents going back to the 18th century, and in doing so have been more impressed with them than we ought. A closer look is, in my judgement, overdue.

Protection

Much emphasis is placed on protection but little on what we, or the patient, ought to be protected from. For while there is little doubt that we need protection from physical violence and actions that damage property, should we be protected from socially disruptive behaviour, or actions that produce mere dislike? Mental patients often behave in bizarre and socially unpleasant ways; should we claim protection from these? Should we protect mental patients from themselves, that is, from actions which may include risky and unwise ventures or the like?

The modern protection lobbies have been influential, and often we have accepted uncritically their claims. They have found support in the findings from a number of high-profile cases involving fatalities. We have been asked to accept, and rely on, claims that new forms of controls will succeed, without much evidence to support those propositions, except to say that existing arrangements are unsatisfactory. Similarly, we have been asked to rely on clinical judgements about a patient's behaviour, rarely requiring the clinicians to say what 'risk of serious harm' means. Might it not be time that we had answers to those questions? If not, we should at least agree on a set of criteria, which requires those proposing new controls to base their demands on behavioural criteria; that is to say, how many homicides or assaults they expect this or that measure to reduce. The onus would be placed on those seeking change to justify the controls presented, in a manner which allows scrutiny. One could go further; we could demand to know which behavioural criteria are relevant to this or that proposal.

Nor is it clear whether such matters should be left to civil jurisdictions. Dangerous mental patients, capable of causing 'risk of serious harm' have, I suggest, moved beyond the purview of the civil law. If their behaviour is so serious, might that be a matter for the criminal law and the criminal courts? We are close to creating what Brenda Hoggett called that new type of non-criminal crime, a crime of antisocial behaviour, but not a crime dealt with under criminal jurisdictions. I agree with Brenda Hoggett; we should be wary of such a move.

Treatment

In order to be detained under the 1983 Act, the patient must have a mental disorder 'of a nature and degree that warrants detention'. Clinicians are not required to spell out that 'nature or degree', nor are they required to state the patient's ability to make decisions about treatment. The assumption has been that where the patient is sufficiently disordered to be compulsorily detained, then he is incapable of making decisions about treatment. (The Percy Commission had no place for the competent refuser, and did not consider questions of mental capacity to be relevant.) Yet, as noted in Chapter 1, recent research in America (Grisso and Appelbaum 1998) and an examination of mental capacity by the Law Commission (1995) in Britain have cast doubt on that presumption. As a result, a number of cherished beliefs and favoured assumptions about mental disorder have been undermined.

Grisso and Appelbaum (1998) have shown that patients may be psychotic, seriously depressed, or in a moderately advanced stage of dementia, and yet remain competent to make decisions. Leaving aside the empirical evidence to support Grisso and Appelbaum, and accepting that mental capacity and mental disorder are not one and the same, we need to ask how this should affect compulsion. On the face of it, the short answer must be, a great deal, although how and in what way remains unclear. To complicate matters further, Grisso and Appelbaum talk of fluctuations in the levels of competency which, they say, should be noted and assessed.

If patients are able to decide about treatment, then on the face of it there is a case for saying that there is no reason to detain them. If they are able to decide on treatment, then it is reasonable to assume that they can make competent decisions about other matters. But can and should that assumption be made? But which of these 'other matters' are the most important as far as compulsory detention is concerned? One can imagine a situation where the patient is competent to decide on treatment, yet not competent to cope with members of the community and so poses a threat to public safety. Should he be detained? If he is, then is not this an example of mental health legislation providing preventative detention? It seems mightily close to it, when the demands of public safety appear to take precedence over all else. We enter then that murky world where compulsion has more to do with social control than with the medical needs of the patients, in which case we are getting close to the non-criminal crime suggested above. If not, then one can expect questions to be raised about the usefulness of compulsion generally, for if legislation fails to protect us from those who would harm us then what use is it? This type of question has become central to the current debate.

The committee concerned with reviewing the 1983 Mental Health Act (Richardson 1999) spent a great deal of time on the matter of competency, clearly recognising its complexity. The problem the committee faced was to respect patient autonomy, and, by definition, acknowledge the patient's capacity to make decisions, yet find a solution acceptable to clinicians as compatible with best practice. Strangely enough, it seemed not to be concerned about public safety. It proposed three models of care which are set out below.

1   To permit detention in hospital with the offer of treatment but to allow the patient to refuse any medication or other treatment which would require cooperation. The expectation would be that the patient, being exposed to prolonged negotiation and encouragement on the part of the clinical team, would eventually 'consent' to the offered treatment. If the patient lost capacity an application could be made to a tribunal to vary the order.
2   To permit the tribunal to approve a treatment plan allowing treatment despite a capable refusal in certain carefully defined circumstances. This would offer less support to patient autonomy but might more readily gain the approval of clinicians, carers and the families of patients.
3   To allow the capable patient to be free from the administration of medication in the absence of consent for the duration of a preliminary short compulsory order of, for example, 3 months. If during that period the clinical team believed that the patient might have lost capacity they could apply for a variation of the order. After the expiry of the preliminary order the tribunal could approve an order

with treatment despite the patient's capable refusal. The treatment would then fall to be regulated by the safeguards described above. (pp. 40–1)

With the exception of 1, these models do not meet the question posed above, which is about whether some areas of competency are more relevant to decisions about compulsion than others. Put another way, they do not consider which aspects should be taken into account by clinicians before making a compulsory order. If a patient is competent to decide about treatment but not competent to decide how to take care of himself, is that sufficient? If a patient is competent to make decisions about his treatment, and is able to take care of himself but is not competent to make decisions about coping with, say, his financial affairs, what then? The answer is, no one knows. For my part, I can only suggest that the models listed above fail to meet the complexity of the situation. What is needed are models which identify the competencies which are lacking in the patient and which should be taken into account when making a compulsory order, and those which are present but of no consequence. For example, a patient may not be competent to take care of himself but remains competent to speak a foreign language. The competency to speak a foreign language seems irrelevant to the task in hand but the competency to take care of himself is relevant. These are the sort of models we should be producing, for these are directly relevant to decisions about compulsion and entry to compulsory care.

However, the whole question of competency may fizzle out like a damp squib. Some psychiatrists doubt if there are more than a handful of patients who fall into the compulsory detention category yet retain the capacity to decide about treatment. Those that do, say the psychiatrists, will invariably be patients diagnosed as having depression or having a personality disorder – the latter an unwelcome group anyway and unlikely to be detained under present circumstances. These psychiatrists see the debate as interesting yet largely manufactured by academics with too much time on their hands. They point to the practical reality of a huge shortage of beds and an equally large shortage of psychiatrists and resources. They suspect that few psychiatrists will bother taking this type of patient into hospital, that is, those who remain competent to decide about treatment, just to keep them in for lengthy periods without giving treatment, or until the patients make up their minds about treatment or a tribunal overrules them. One can see their point. But this debate ought not to go away; it *is* important and needs consideration from practitioners and others alike. It requires a new way of thinking and a willingness to ask new questions.

To prevent discrimination on the basis of a psychiatric classification

The third of Gostin's strategies need not concern us here for this has been dealt with earlier where the importance of defining the terms used in legislation was pointed out. Gostin is opposed to the practice of using open-ended terminology and in this he is entirely correct.

Conclusion

In this chapter, the aim has been to seek justifications for compulsory detention, using the framework provided by Larry Gostin called 'the ideology of entitlement'. Generally speaking, little consideration appears to have been given to the question about justifying compulsion, and we appear to have taken it for granted that compulsory admissions are an acceptable part of mental health law. We seem to have acknowledged that few changes need to be made to existing procedures, so that further debate is, if not unwelcome, unnecessary, and, if the extent of research is anything to go by, that would seem to be correct.

Traditionally, compulsory powers have been justified in the following ways. First, on the basis that some form of mental disorder be present 'of a nature or degree that warrants compulsion', where the patient's condition can be determined clinically according to current diagnostic knowledge. Second, justifications have been made on the basis of what I have called 'other conditions' of which three are identified. First, that which comes under the general heading of *parens patriae*, second, the right to treatment, and finally on the basis of public safety. I suggest that these so-called 'other conditions' are not discrete, there is much overlap; nor do they cover the entire debate. As a further complication, they have sometimes been called upon to provide a justification in their own right. However, more usually, these 'other conditions' have been presented as a composite package. So, for example, supporters of the right to treatment have never claimed it was a sufficient justification of itself to detain a person in a mental hospital, there had to be a danger to the patient and/or to others as well. Similarly, for those justifying compulsion on *parens patriae* grounds, they have never wanted to claim this was sufficient of itself, and have included other criteria such as levels of dangerousness.

I have tried to show that there are severe limitations to those justifications. None have proved satisfactory or able to stand alone; at best they are partial justifications for what is, after all, a complex matter. They are partial in two senses; first, that this type of legislation has

always been backed by a multitude of ethical and practical considerations, and has never relied on a single justification, and second, that
more often than not the best one can do is to identify strands which have
appeared from time to time in the debates surrounding compulsion.
Sometimes these strands have been stronger at certain periods than at
others and sometimes hardly discernible. But they always seem to
reappear, albeit in a slightly different form. The next step is to consider
questions of procedures, including an examination of the key players
and their legislative duties. This is the aim in Chapter 3.

3

Doctors, Social Workers and Relatives

Writing in 1980 about the way the 1959 Mental Health Act operated, I thought that the procedures for deciding and detaining a patient for compulsory admission had not worked well (Bean 1980). GPs and social workers rarely knew their duties, rarely knew the law and rarely offered much by way of assistance to the psychiatrists – frankly, the GPs did what they were told. When the social workers disagreed with the psychiatrists, they were invariably outmanoeuvred into having to accept the psychiatrist's opinion (ibid. 1980). There have been changes since then; the 1959 Act has been replaced by the 1983 Act, social workers are now required to be Approved, that is, they have to complete a recognised training programme, and GPs are said to be rather better trained than hitherto in their knowledge of mental health legislation. But have these changes greatly affected things? Has the 1983 Act improved the social worker and GP input, and has the training improved procedures? The answer is, probably yes, at least in some respects, but we do not know for certain; unfortunately what has not changed has been the amount of research, which still remains unacceptably small.

All societies are faced with questions about the appropriate proced-ures for compulsory hospital admissions, and their solutions are legion. They all seem to involve the medical profession but some also use the local police, some the patients' relatives, and some local officials such as the mayor. In Britain, we use the medical profession, social workers and the patients' relatives, and in this we are almost unique. Under the 1959 Act, social workers were called Mental Welfare Officers, who were themselves a later version of the Poor Law Relieving Officer first used under Section 20 of the 1744 Vagrancy Act (Bean 1980, p. 221). They had to take charge of any patient found wandering at large and bring him to a Justice of the Peace (JP).

Two questions dominate: who is to make the decisions, and who should be responsible for transporting the patient to a hospital? The latter is not unimportant, for those who do the transporting usually have other tasks such as gaining access to mentally disordered people living in the community, or apprehending absconders. Within the first question, there are subsidiary questions such as where is the decision to be made, that is, in a hospital or police station, and what safeguards are to be provided to protect the patients against overzealous decision-makers? Then there are questions about the involvement of any judicial authority – this can be linked to the suggestion that we introduce a formal right of appeal. Questions surrounding judicial authority will be dealt with first.

Judicial authority

The argument for introducing judicial authority is that compulsory care involves an infringement of personal liberty, even if its purpose is to provide care that the patient would not otherwise receive. A detained patient has no right to refuse treatment, although he retains his common law right not to be assaulted or subjected to coercive and intrusive measures. Gronwell (1985, p. 254) says that in Sweden:

> politicians and lawyers have very light-heartedly left it to the psychiatrists alone to deal with these very difficult situations [but because] compulsory admission and treatment of a very sick person means a deprivation of liberty and an infringement of privacy it makes the decisions a real concern also for politicians and lawyers.

Are we in Britain also guilty of 'light-heartedly leaving the matter to psychiatrists', and, if so, is it not time we reopened the debate?

Judicial authorities were involved in compulsory admissions in Britain up to the 1959 Act, originally as part of their duties under the Poor Law, whether as administrators of the asylum, or by their authority to order the detention of dangerous lunatics. Later, they became part of the so-called certification process which involved interviewing a patient in his own home, or in hospital, acting on *ex parte* statements, and sitting as a civil court. The Percy Commission (1957) recommended that the existing judicial authority be removed for the standard compulsory admissions to hospital. It was retained where physicians and social workers were 'met with overriding objections from relatives to a compulsory order', and under Section 135 of the 1983 Act where an application had to be made to a court for a social worker to enter premises where it was believed a mentally disordered patient may reside and was not being cared for.

The Percy Commission did not believe that the court was a proper authority to deal with medical matters, and did not think that the courts had the necessary expertise to make informed decisions about mental disorder. The Commission thought that the courts presented an illusion of authority, and by their presence criminalised a medical non-criminal process. The Commission's views were a logical extension of the theoretical position adopted throughout their Report, supported by the evidence of a number of witnesses, who stressed that the decisions about whether the patient should or should not be compelled to enter hospital turned mainly on the diagnosis of his mental condition. These, it was said, were medical matters, about which it was difficult for a non-medical person to have an opinion. If a check on the opinion of a certifying doctor was needed, they suggested it would be better to have a second medical opinion rather than one from a JP (Percy Commission 1957, para. 267). This has to be set against those who saw certification as other than a medical matter, a position succinctly stated by the Justices Clerks Society in their evidence to the Percy Commission:

> There is not a single exception in times of peace to that well established principle of our common law that a man may not be put under restraint save by due powers of law as signified by the order of a judicial authority... Any attempt to dispense with the intervention of the magistrates in these matters would in our view, be an encroachment of that principle. (quoted in Bean 1980, p. 16)

There were numerous criticisms of the way the courts functioned under their certification procedures. The most persistent one was that the hearings were scarcely more than a formality, with the magistrates accepting uncritically the medical officers' views – magistrates, it was said, lacked the knowledge to challenge the physician. Moreover, the court was said to criminalise proceedings about what should be a medical matter. The point was made by one witness that as a court was not required to determine whether a patient should or should not be treated for appendicitis, why then for a mental illness? The Percy Commission thought it was difficult to make patients believe that the court was there to protect their civil rights: courts were too closely associated with criminal matters for that point to be accepted. Accordingly, the role of the court was, according to the Percy Commission, an unnecessary and unwarranted intrusion on what should, after all, be a matter undertaken by medical men. Where safeguards were needed, they could be provided by other medical men, or by other medical specialists.

The debate hinges on a dispute between *medicine versus the law*, or *medical treatment versus civil liberties*; that is, a clash between the interests of the patient against the protection of the patient's civil rights. Reconciling that conflict is difficult; one group emphasises rights, the rule of law and the importance of the judiciary as a guardian of liberties, and the other sees mental disorder as the prerogative of the medical profession. It is about whether we trust psychiatrists, or whether we believe that non-medical persons, acting according to judicial authority, are better able to protect us against the excesses of these professionals. In vain do psychiatrists protest that the debate is locked into a set of 19th-century fears when medical men had to be restrained from railroading patients into mental hospitals. They say these fears are outdated, if only because there is now a desperate shortage of mental hospital beds, and an equally desperate shortage of psychiatrists to carry out the treatment. No psychiatrist is going to railroad patients into hospital who do not need to be there, or treat patients who cannot be treated, or are unwilling to accept psychiatric help. Other patients will be more deserving of their time and expertise.

There is a danger of using 19th-century arguments for a 21st-century problem. Perhaps we have little to fear from overzealous psychiatrists nowadays: in my own research conducted in the late 1970s, it was the psychiatrists who were more reluctant to use the compulsory powers, and acted against the advice of social workers, relatives and GPs who asked for patients to be compulsorily admitted (ibid. 1980). To the civil libertarian that is not the point: the power granted to psychiatrists to make an order, even for only one patient, is sufficient to demand justification; the number of patients detained is not the issue.

There has been no call to include the courts, or to introduce supervision by judicial authority. Yet civil libertarians, who have opposed the introduction of additional controls, find themselves vindicated whenever they find evidence of malpractice, as occurred when one health authority placed a large number of patients on its Supervision Register to bolster its chances of claiming extra resources, suggesting it needed additional help to cope with difficult patients. The patients had become political tools, where their civil rights were usurped in order to bring financial benefit to the authority. These types of infringement raise again the spectre of the railroading psychiatrists; who, if not railroading patients into hospital, are railroading them onto community controls. Faced with such cynical disregard for patients' rights, civil libertarians justifiably ask whether mental health professionals can ever be trusted.

The right of appeal

The stark contrasts of the legal versus treatment dichotomy may not turn out to be so stark after all. Might there not be ways in which the courts could be involved without seeking to undermine the medical and allied professions position? That is, could not legislation provide a right of appeal against a compulsory order, whether for hospital or community supervision? A court would hear that appeal. The advantages are clear; the court is an independent authority, it encourages openness by making its decisions public, the patient would have a right to plead, to be represented, argue his case and examine the evidence. The court stands in contrast to the mental health services where decisions are administrative and secretive – with the Supervised Discharge Order an application is made by a medical officer to the health authority in which he works, hardly an example of independent scrutiny. Is not this an area where the courts could make a contribution? There are no provisions in the Act or in the regulations for a right of appeal. The 1983 Act allows the detained patient to appeal to a Mental Health Review Tribunal (MHRT), but only after admission, and invariably after treatment. There is no appeal prior to admission, that is, no appeal against the decision to admit, and no appeal against a decision to be placed under supervision or placed on a Supervision Register. The administrative requirements would be complicated, and the procedures demanding but that should not stop them being considered.

An appeal would need to be heard before admission (or before the patient was placed on supervision) and before treatment is given. If the appeal was heard after treatment, the impact of the patient's case might be lost, the treatment might distort the patient's condition, or prevent the patient giving his point of view. Appeals could work something like this. For an appeal against a Supervised Discharge Order the hearing could be held either in court, or in hospital – the patient could decide – at some point prior to the order being made. The patient could hear the evidence, be represented – or if not legally represented, then be able to call on the services of a support person, perhaps a social worker. Similarly, the court could call on the services of a psychiatrist, who could act as an advisor. The support person could advise on procedures and so on, and offset any advantage gained by the prosecution who could call on the expertise of the psychiatrist. The courts could accept or refuse the appeal.

For an appeal against a Compulsory Hospital Order, matters become more complex. Emergencies take place throughout the 24 hours, often at night: if the appeal is to be meaningful it must take place before treatment is given. That means detaining the patient in a place of safety until the hearing – it is suggested for no more than 12 hours. Treatment could be given in exceptional circumstances and only of a minimal amount so as not to affect the patient's ability to conduct an appeal.

Whether an appeal system could work or not depends on the political will to see it through. One could imagine what the objections might be: that an appeal is unnecessary; that appeals have not been needed before so why introduce them now; that the case for introducing appeals has not been made; that the procedures are too cumbersome and overbureaucratised. (Worse still, that an appeal is inappropriate because the patient is unable to make a decision as his mental disorder renders him unable to do so – the existence of the mental disorder is precisely what the court is to decide.) Set against these are ethical and political considerations concerned with the rights of the mentally disordered. Lars Gronwall (1985, p. 254) says of Sweden that 'society takes a very heavy responsibility for the patient's well-being by permitting compulsory care', adding that this makes it important for legal security to be augmented, with the rights of the mentally ill strengthened (ibid. p. 257). He says that a court or other judicial body should take the responsibility for compulsory admissions rather than psychiatrists – in this context taking responsibility means giving the court powers to sit as an appeal court.

The Report of the Expert Committee on the 1983 Act did not see the need for an appeal prior to admission, or rather they did not appear to consider it (Richardson 1999). Instead they proposed the appointment of an Independent Reviewer, who would probably be a legal member of the newly designated MHRT, who would review the patient's case after seven days under an existing order. That is, the patient would have been admitted and almost certainly been given treatment, probably of a serious nature. The Review would not, however, appear to be very exhaustive:

> We do not however wish to introduce an automatic oral hearing at this stage and would envisage the review as essentially a paper or electronic exercise. [We want] to introduce an early safeguard for patients which is of sufficient independence and status to inspire confidence and at the same time as undemanding as possible in terms of extra resources. (ibid. para. 5.83)

That Independent Review will be expected to take place after day seven of a Compulsory Assessment Order (which could involve compulsory treatment) which will end unless the care team applies on paper to the Independent Reviewer to confirm a provisional 21-day order. The Independent Reviewer may: (a) confirm the 21-day order, (b) call for more information, and (c) call for an expedited MHRT. The proposal is that the Independent Reviewer is likely to be a lawyer on the MHRT.

Whether so or not, this seems another example of a missed set of opportunities, and a nudge, but only a nudge, in the direction of providing a proper appeals procedure. What is needed is an appeal *before* admission not *after*, for by that time all the civil rights questions have been ignored (the right to be represented, to argue one's case, to be free of treatment until found to be justifiably detained by a judicial authority, to have the case against the patient made available to the patient before a decision is made, and so on), and the patients placed in a position where it is much more difficult to argue their case, especially after admission, and after treatment. Of course, those supporting this proposal would say it all depends on the enthusiasm of the Independent Reviewer, but as the proposal stands a little more adventure on behalf of the Review Committee and a little more concern for the patient's rights may have been more of the order of the day.

The doctor's part in the procedure

The doctor's legal position under the 1983 Act is set out neatly by Brenda Hoggett (1984, p. 95). To paraphrase:

- Applications for admissions to hospital under Section 2 (for assessment) or Section 3 (for treatment) or for reception into guardianship under Section 7 must be supported by the recommendations of two doctors (Sections 2(3), 3(3) and 7(3)).
- An application for assessment in an emergency under Section 4 requires the support of only one doctor (Section 4(3)).
- A warrant under Section 135(1) to gain entry to private premises and remove the patient to a place of safety can only be executed if a doctor is present (Section 135(4)) although the patient can be taken to hospital without any formal recommendation.
- Whenever the 1983 Act requires the recommendation of two doctors, one of them must be on the list of those approved under Section 12(2).

In addition, the police are given powers to remove a person from a public place to a place of safety under Section 136. (See Chapter 5 where a discussion of Section 136 considers these police powers.) Once the patient is in a place of safety, a physician and a social worker are called to conduct an examination.

The doctor's task is to make the medical recommendation which is then submitted to the appropriate hospital authority. The Percy Commission recommended that the procedures should not require certificates ('certification' had become a pejorative term); instead there should be medical recommendations containing the doctor's opinion stating that the patient satisfies the necessary criteria (para. 375). The suggestions from the Percy Commission were incorporated in the 1959 Act and largely retained under the 1983 Act. The Percy Commission (1957) added that 'we trust that the term "certification", and all that is associated with it will fall completely into disuse' (para. 377).

The Percy Commission (1957) viewed the medical recommendation as pivotal. It wanted to place matters in the hands of those with knowledge and experience needed to form sound judgements (para. 390). The Commission considered it 'inappropriate for a person who is not medically qualified to be required to state an opinion on the patients' state of mind and need for care and treatment' (para. 390). This was a dig at the magistrates. Social workers had a part to play – 'Medical and non-medical opinions should supplement each other' – but not at an equal level, for 'each person should be expected to contribute to the final decision only what is appropriate to his own knowledge or experience, or of his relationship with the patient' (ibid. para. 390). Social workers could make their contribution but it would be less than the physician.

There are few in Britain nowadays who would disagree with the prominence given to medical personnel, except perhaps a small group of anti-psychiatrists who question the existence of mental disorder and the position of psychiatrists. These apart, questions still arise about the procedures; for example, why is a single doctor required for an emergency admission for observation and two doctors required to make recommendations for an admission for treatment. The Percy Commission wanted one doctor to be experienced in the diagnosis or treatment of mental disorder – what we now call a physician approved under Section 12(2) of the 1983 Act who may or may not be a psychiatrist, and the other doctor should be the GP with detailed knowledge of the patient including family history and background. The psychiatrist would offer specialist knowledge, the GP a generalist: presumably one acting as a corrective to the other.

Does such a system work? From research in the late 1970s, it was clear that two doctors rarely operated in the way suggested by the Percy Commission (Bean 1980). The psychiatrists ran the programme; they had the expertise, the status and the access to the resources. GPs are relatively lowly figures in a medical hierarchy where high status is given according to specialist knowledge. Accordingly, GPs were not encouraged to dispute psychiatric opinions, the more so if the psychiatrists were consultants. Moreover, the psychiatrists had greater knowledge of the law, and invariably had more experience dealing with psychiatric emergencies, but most of all they had the resources to provide treatment – all of which gave them a powerful advantage over their medical colleagues.

Times have changed since the Percy Commission in ways which additionally disadvantage the GP. Nowadays, the second doctor is unlikely to be the patient's GP; he may be a locum, or a doctor from another GP practice, or one employed to undertake emergency services at the request of the local GP. Paradoxically, the second doctor may know less about the patient than the psychiatrist. We have created an illusion of a corrective, a pretence almost, where the second doctor's contribution is likely to be less than expected – at least in most urban areas – and not always offering much in the way of background information.

Might it not be time to take a more honest approach and remove the illusion? Why not accept the reality that the psychiatrist is the dominant figure and give him sole responsibility – or to a Section 12(2) doctor – to act alone? If the aim was to require one doctor to check on the other, then things have not worked out that way. Would the patient object to such changes, and would these changes affect the number and type of admissions? Probably not, for the psychiatrist would continue to make decisions as before, and it is doubtful if the patient would be concerned about such procedural changes anyway.

(I have dealt only with the main features of the legislation, but it is more complex than this. For example, the rules aimed at securing the doctor's independence are such that the two doctors cannot be partners, they cannot be related, nor can one be the assistant of the other. Nor can any recommending doctor be related to the patient, so that as Brenda Hoggett puts it, 'these rules do an excellent job in ensuring that a psychiatrist does not conspire with his assistant to place his wife in a mental nursing home which he runs' (1984, p. 99). And there are additional restrictions under the 1983 Act which prohibit *both* doctors on the hospital staff producing the recommendations if one is under the direction of the other. The exception is when getting an outside doctor would cause serious delay involving *serious* risk to the patient's health or safety. These are to be welcomed, for there are good reasons for preventing a doctor recommending the admission of a close relative or someone who is his private patient.)

For admission for assessment, that is, not treatment, Section 4 of the 1983 Act permits one medical recommendation from any qualified physician – the physician does not have to be a Section 12(2) doctor – plus an application from a social worker or relative. The physician must have examined the patient within a specified period of time (Section 12(1)). In practice and with so few beds available, it is unlikely the physician will be a junior houseman from a local hospital, even if a relative or social worker was prepared to make the application. The consultant psychiatrist of the respective hospital would almost certainly have to agree to the patient being admitted. Again one wonders if the so-called emergency admission for observation involving one doctor, any qualified doctor, and a social worker or relative is acceptable, and I say this while recognising that the Richardson Committee have made proposals for changing these admission sections. (I have never known a case where a patient admitted for assessment is not treated: it is most unlikely that having gone through the business of making a Compulsory Assessment Order the patient will only be observed for a given period of time.) Might it not be time to grasp that particular nettle too and require a consultant psychiatrist or Section 12(2) doctor to make the recommendation, and instead of having a three-day order make it a seven-day order, allowing treatment to be given? In the past, the objection has been that to provide treatment an MHRT must hear any appeal, and three days is too short to arrange an tribunal. Were the appeal procedures introduced as suggested above, there would be no need for the tribunal.

I am suggesting that the time has come to review these procedures. Times have changed and events moved on and, while existing legislation might have been appropriate for earlier times, it is less so now. It is time to update procedures and bring them in line with modern requirements. However, the Review Committee, without a great deal of discussion, simply stated that there should be two 'other professionals', that is, two physicians who should be (a) one medical practitioner, usually a psychiatrist from the Trust providing specialist mental health services, with accredited training under the new Act, and (b) one other mental health professional who is either specifically trained or has knowledge of the patient. No suggestion of change here, in fact no suggestion of anything that remotely challenges existing thinking. Again, a lost opportunity if ever there was one.

The social workers and relatives

Under Section 11(1) of the 1983 Act, applications for compulsory admissions to mental hospitals, whether for assessment or treatment, may be made either by an Approved Social Worker (ASW) or by the patient's nearest relative. The so-called application is a curious feature of the legislation – it is an application to the managers of the hospital to admit the patient under a compulsory order. Without that application there is no authority to detain. On the face of it, the applicant is in a very powerful position, although in practice that may be less so. Why is an application required?

The Percy Commission (1957) wanted the relatives to be the key figures:

> Ideally in our view the application should be made by a relative of the patient on medical recommendation, with a mental welfare officer available to explain the procedure and provide the application form and to transport the patient to hospital if necessary. (para. 403)

In practice, the relative rarely makes the application, the professionalisation of social work in the 1960s had no place for the amateur, and relatives were not often asked to assist (Bean 1980). Under the 1983 Act, Section 11(1) says applications for compulsory admission to hospital made for assessment or treatment can be made by either the patients nearest relative or the ASW (the order is instructive): that is to say, the ASW cannot prevent the relative from making the application, and the relative cannot prevent the ASW doing likewise. If, however, the relative makes the application, he must rely on the ASW for assistance – usually in the form of guidance and information (the ASW carries the application forms). The ASW must convey the patient to hospital irrespective of who makes the application. Where the patient is admitted for treatment on a long-term order, the ASW *must* consult the nearest relative (the nearest relative is defined as beginning with the husband/wife and moving downwards in status).

Involving the relative is a way of recognising the importance of kinship, where the relative is expected to protect the patient from any forms of malpractice including the railroading doctor. In spite of the many changes that have taken place and with fewer expectations of railroading, there remain good reasons to consult the relative – consultation, of course, differs from direct involvement. Relatives have a right to know how and under what circumstances decisions are made and have the right to object to matters not in their or the patient's interest. An interesting question is whether any objection should be overruled by the ASW. Unfortunately the law is silent on this matter.

Before an ASW makes an application for admission to hospital, the ASW must:

interview the patient in a suitable manner and satisfy himself that detention in a hospital is, in all the circumstances of the case, the most appropriate way of providing the care and medical treatment of which the patient stands in need. (1983 Act, Section 13(2))

Brenda Hoggett says:

This is a most welcome recognition of the professional contribution which a properly trained social worker has to make, although it has a slightly hollow ring when the contribution can easily be avoided by getting the relative to apply instead. (1984, p. 85)

But is it a 'welcome recognition'? Does it not leave unclear the basic question; what is the social worker's position and what is the social worker's contribution? An attendant question about whether that position is still required also needs to be asked.

The 1983 Act gives the social worker the right to refuse to make the application. In the application the social worker must confirm the procedural details, and satisfy himself that detention in hospital is the most appropriate way of providing the care and medical treatment which the patient needs. It does not ask the social worker to evaluate that care, nor does it permit the social worker to be involved in any subsequent treatment. The social worker's task ends at the point at which he has conveyed the patient to the hospital. (There is more involvement in the Supervised Discharged Order.)

Brenda Hoggett says it is essential for practitioners to confront the issue of what is properly a medical problem, a social problem, or a mixture of both (ibid. p. 104). It is suggested that a medical problem centres on the decision to admit, compulsorily or not. It may not be necessary to be certain about the diagnosis, which can and often does change after treatment, but it will be necessary to show that the psychiatric condition 'is of a nature and degree' that warrants compulsory care. In contrast, social problems centre on the patient's background, previous social history, family relationships and so on. These are less important when faced with a floridly psychotic person posing a risk to self or others. Social problems may be eased by information on the patient's background, but are not vital to the decision.

Social problems may include decisions about where the patient should be detained, and where to receive treatment. The family may be prepared to keep the patient at home, or may want local specialist nursing facilities. They need to be consulted about these, and the social worker's contribution will be valued; knowledge of local or national facilities is always worthwhile. Transporting the patient to that institution, or arranging transport is another necessary social activity. All are important, but are not adequate justifications for retaining the social worker formally in the admission procedure.

Social workers claim that they not only deal with the patients' social problems but also protect the patients' rights and interests against the psychiatrists. There are numerous anecdotal accounts in which the social worker objected to the use of compulsion and persuaded the psychiatrist not to make an order, and these may well be true. There are, however, as many where the social worker objected and the objections came to nothing, or wanted a compulsory order but the psychiatrist refused. The evidence that social workers protect patients' rights and act in the patients' best interests or protect the patients against the unwelcome decisions of psychiatrists is rarely forthcoming. There is no doubt that some consultation may be helpful but this is different from supporting an active legal involvement. Those wanting to retain the social worker's role argue that the social worker acts as a brake on the overenthusiastic psychiatrist but again the evidence for this, except anecdotal, is not forthcoming. To repeat the point; psychiatrists nowadays do not railroad, they are more intent on keeping patients out than pulling them in. Conveying the patient to the hospital, however, should remain part of the social worker's task but, in my judgement, the time has arrived where the application in its present legal form is redundant. It could be replaced by a requirement that the social worker be consulted before any medical recommendation is made, but not involved further in the patient's detention. Introducing a right of appeal further weakens the case for retaining the social worker and the application.

The Expert Committee (Department of Health 1999) considered the social worker's position and concluded that the ASW be retained as the applicant. It then added, somewhat surprisingly, that 'consideration be given to the gradual extension of the role of the applicant to include other mental health professionals who are not psychiatrists'. Presumably this means psychologists and so on. But why? In my view the aim is to reduce the involvement of professional groups not increase them, if only because the rights of the patient seem more important than those of the professsionals. We ought not to be led to the view that competency to decide on procedures equates with a right to undertake those procedures, yet that is what the Expert Committee seem to be saying. If so, this sets a dangerous precedent. The reasons for retaining the ASW or rather the reasons put to the Committee for retaining the ASW were:

(a) despite the increasing move towards integrated management, social workers retain an important element of independence, not least because they bring a non-medical perspective to bear, and independence remains an essential requirement;

(b) social workers perform an important co-ordinating role both before and after the assessment and typically deal with the social and domestic implications of an individual's admission to compulsion;

(c) social workers receive specific and rigorous training for the role. (Department of Health 1999, paras 5.7–5.13)

The Committee says it appreciates that for some these arguments are not very powerful (para. 512), as indeed they are not. Consideration needs to be given to a different set of assumptions, not based on a view that the application is necessary unless stated otherwise, but on the alternative, that the applicant's position should be under scrutiny and assumed redundant unless proven necessary. The Committee did not adopt that reductionist view, but appeared too eager to appease other professional groups. As things are it still needs to be stated why an application is needed.

Abandoning the social work application is unlikely to be popular in many circles let alone social work ones. Yet there has always been a presumption in English law that those involved in taking away liberties have the onus placed on them to justify their position. Where is the evidence that social workers protect patients' rights? Where is the evidence that they act as a restraining influence on the psychiatrist? Where is the evidence that the social worker's role produces a more efficient and more humane compulsory admission procedure? The answer, sadly, is that little evidence is available, yet without more, there remains some difficulty in knowing why those procedures should be retained, and the onus must be on those undertaking the restraints to show otherwise.

Detaining voluntary patients

Patients entering hospital as voluntary patients can, under Section 5 of the 1983 Act, be detained for up to 72 hours on a so-called holding power under Section 5(2) of the 1983 Act. A registered medical practitioner is given that power. Section 5(4) of the Act can be used when Section 5(2) cannot be operated because no physician is available. Section 5(4) allows a patient to be detained by a nurse for up to 6 hours (see also Bean and Mounser 1993, p. 83). These powers have always been contentious, and remain so. The original justification for Section

5(2) goes back to the 1959 Act, where a holding power was given under Section 30(2) to prevent patients leaving hospital against medical advice where their condition was considered unsuitable for them to do so. The holding power is there so that a full assessment can be made later to determine whether an order under another section is required. A suspicion, fostered under the 1959 Act and retained under the 1983 Act, is that this holding power is used as a way of bypassing the requirements of Sections 2 and 3. That is to say, it is being used as a detaining section so that once in the hospital the patient can be detained and any required documentation dealt with later. And why the nurse under Section 5(4)? The official reason was that it provided back-up when no physicians were available, although the unofficial reason is that it was a sop to COHSE (the nursing union) to help secure cooperation to run the 1983 Act. A more charitable view is that nurses have always had common law powers and when linked to their duty of care they had little guidance as to their duty and liability – Section 5(4) provides that.

Unfortunately, there is little or no data on how these sections work. In a study in 1986, some information was produced showing that these holding arrangements were being abused (ibid. p. 85) where:

> social control is being extended to the wider group including the multidisciplinary team who are gradually coming to have more and more powers in line with the medical model which they appear to emulate (ibid. p. 85)

That is to say, about 90% of all applications made under Section 5(2) were by junior doctors, with only 10.8% made by consultants. When asked why they used Section 5(2), some psychiatrists said it was in order to gain the cooperation of the patients, and to allow section papers to be obtained – 96.1% of patients under Section 5(2) were originally admitted informally. Only half those on Section 5(2) 'were being converted to another section', which at the very least seemed to contravene the spirit of the Act, for Section 5(2) was intended as a holding power before a Section 2 or 3 admission was to be made (ibid. p. 86).

More recently, the Mental Health Act Commission (MHAC) has been critical of the way Section 5(2) has been used. For 1995/96, there were 10,600 detentions made under Section 5(2), with wide variations between units. The MHAC says a ratio of 1 Section 5(2) to every 4 Section 2 or 3 would be unusually high – it does not give a ratio it would regard as acceptable – but Thameside Trust reported a ratio of 29:107. The MHAC drew attention 'to an unacceptably high proportion of detentions under Section 5(2) in which assessments are delayed or the time limit allowed to expire without any record of assessment having begun' (Mental Health Act Commission 1997, p. 47). The Notes for Guidance in the Code of Practice (8.1.b) require that 'the patient should be assessed as speedily as possible' (quoted in ibid. p. 47).

There is no information in the Seventh Biennial Report of the MHAC on these holding powers. The Eighth Biennial Report, however, provides a full discussion, noting that the use of Section 5(4) and Section 5(2) has continued to increase: for Section 5(4) from 770 in 1987/88 to 1616 in 1997/98 and for Section 5(2) from 5,372 in 1987/88 to 9,706 in 1997/98, these at a time when compulsory admissions generally are falling (Mental Health Act Commission 1997/99, p. 72) (but see the debate in Chapter 2 on the numbers of patients thought to be detained). The MHAC noted with concern, however, that the Act is sometimes invoked only when the patient attempts to leave or resist treatment, and that proper assessments may only be undertaken at that point. The MHAC added a reminder that the purpose of the holding powers is to prevent the patients from leaving the ward *only* until they can be assessed for further detention, which means that assessment must be completed as soon as possible and not be allowed to lapse after 72 hours (for Section 5(2)). The patient should be discharged from detention under the section as soon as it is decided that formal admission will not be necessary. The MHAC noted a general improvement in the speed of implementing a full assessment, but still came across instances where the section has been prolonged for purposes other than that of completing an assessment (ibid. p. 81).

There is still the question as to why the holding powers were introduced, especially Section 5(4), for how can it be justified that a nurse, however well qualified, be allowed to take away a patient's liberty, albeit for six hours? Moreover, what effect does that have on the patient's view of the nursing profession? Can it really be that there is no physician available to make the order? Crises with patients rarely blow up without warning and, even if they do, how can it be that the responsible physician or his representative is unavailable? Might it not be that the time has come to repeal Section 5(4) and confine the decision to the Responsible Medical Officer, who, as his title suggests, should be responsible?

The issues raised here lead again to those wider questions about the justification for compulsion and how and under what circumstances that should occur. On a more parochial matter, they raise questions about the level of research being conducted in Britain on the way the legislation operates. There is a constant struggle to find data, even of the most elementary kind, concerning the use of these sections in what is, after all, a major piece of legislation – and most of the available data are from the MHAC. The 1983 Mental Health Act has been in operation for a number of years now and we still know little about how the compulsory procedures work, and are reduced to making policy pronouncements on the basis of anecdotal evidence. Questions are raised regularly in the MHAC's reports, and suggestions made for more research, but little comes from it. Research on mental health law appears to be a low priority in Britain but other countries manage it more successfully: why cannot we?

Summary and conclusion

The procedures compelling patients who are non-offenders to go into hospital (or in some circumstances to be placed on a Supervision Register or under a Supervised Discharge Order) consist of recommendations made by one or two doctors, depending on whether admission is for assessment or treatment, and an application to the hospital managers, either by the patient's nearest relative, or by an ASW. Brenda Hoggett (1984, p. 71) comments on the curious features of those procedures: the first is that the physician never has the final word, he cannot force either the relative or the social worker to act. The second is that the final decision can be made either by a detached professional or by a person who is closely involved with the patient.

The aim has been to examine these procedures, and I have done so on the assumption of a reductionist approach to mental health law. On this basis, I have suggested that many need updating and refining. In my judgement, many are outdated, and no longer effective: the medical recommendations do not produce the necessary corrective, and could be done equally well by one doctor, an approved Section 12(2) doctor, preferably a psychiatrist. Similarly, it is doubtful if the application, an historical nicety perhaps, provides an acceptable alternative – a right of appeal would be better.

Changes in mental health legislation occur infrequently, and in the current rush to produce new legislation there is sometimes a reluctance to deal with matters which appear not to be contentious, even if they do not work well. The compulsory admissions procedures are a case in point, where the Expert Committee seemed more interested in coming to cosy conclusions rather than examining the position in detail. The Committee has taken on board the approach of earlier committees where there has been a tendency to use existing powers as a template for other legislation: the 1959 Act from the 1930 Act, the 1983 Act from both, and the Supervised Discharge Order which uses procedures similar to those for compulsory admissions to hospital. I think it would be wrong to leave the present system as it is; it is neither efficient nor effective – other procedures could be introduced which are more so. Changes are likely to be resisted by professionals such as social workers and nurses who will claim that the rights of patients are being neglected, or they will see their loss of authority as a professional slight. Yet the new proposals suggested here would better protect the patient, and, as for losing authority, a lack of authority in law does not mean a lack of authority in practice. Social work and nursing will be judged ultimately on their levels of practice, not on their involvement in the compulsory admission process.

An additional point: the proposals here have been based on the assumption that there is nothing problematic about the place in which the patient is treated. The Percy Commission (1957) did not want legal distinctions between hospitals; it wanted no rigid legal barrier against the admission of any patient to any hospital which provided suitable treatment (para. 378). Its wishes were accepted and translated into legislation (see Section 145(1) of the 1959 Act). Times have changed, and there are fewer old-style hospitals and more and more patients are being treated in private accommodation or local authority hostels. Not all are at the standard one might wish, and, as the MHAC says, they 'do not reflect a policy of good practice', adding that 'many [people] suggest that there is a painful argument in favour of compulsory admission to a mental health service rather than being committed to a defined place such as a hospital or even a hostel' (1993, p. 103). That would seem a dangerous move, and in the wrong direction altogether; identifying and locating who is directly responsible for the patient while under treatment must be a matter of concern. The possibility of a situation arising where responsibility can be avoided, and the patient moved from one accommodation to another opens up possibilities for neglect. Naming the residence and prohibiting a change except in exceptional circumstances would be the way forward, alongside closer inspections of the premises. It would not be wise to encourage a system where institutions were able to transfer patients, especially those who became difficult and awkward to treat. It is much better to insist that the receiving hospital be named in the order.

4

Control in the Community

On 1 January 1994 Supervision Registers were introduced in Britain in accordance with Circular HSG(94)5 (Department of Health 1994). These were part of a so-called wider information system developed by health authority provider units to identify patients known to be at significant risk, or potentially at significant risk, of committing serious violence or suicide, or of serious neglect as a result of severe and enduring mental illness. A year later the Supervised Discharge Order was introduced under the Mental Health (Patients in the Community) Act 1995. Supervision was to be for a limited number of patients who, after being detained in hospital for treatment under the 1983 Act, needed formal supervision to ensure that they received suitable care.

How have we arrived at such a position? That is, why were such controls needed? The standard answer would come from those concerned with community safety, who would say that mental health services have failed a small, but not insignificant, number of persons suffering from mental disorder, in particular schizophrenics who elude, or are not given adequate support in, the community (Exworthy 1995, p. 223). Community care, or rather decarceration, is said to be the cause of the problem, leaving some patients untreated who then 'slip through the net' to become involved in more serious incidents. The Ritchie Report (Ritchie et al. 1994) on *The Care and Treatment of Christopher Clunis* stands out as a beacon for the community safety lobby demanding as it did additional controls. These were to give protection against the violent mentally disordered patient, and were part of a comprehensive community service where compulsory treatment is but one feature.

This standard answer would be a composite answer gleaned from different strands of a complex debate that includes patients' civil rights, the powers of the mental health professionals, community safety and much more. It has many shades and facets. In Britain, community controls are sometimes viewed with suspicion, being seen as representing a new power base for the psychiatric profession; the older one being weakened by the decarceratation movement. Compulsory community controls are, to these critics, not about reducing admissions, or about providing treatment, but about something more sinister – the strengthening of psychiatric power and a subsequent loss of civil rights. However, in the United States, compulsory community provisions are viewed more sympathetically, where compulsory care in the community is seen as acting as a relief from the repressive conditions of many mental hospitals, and therefore a more attractive alternative.

An overview of existing facilities

The two orders described above are part of a more complex system of community controls which include Guardianship (Section 7 of the 1983 Act), extended leave (Section 17) and the Probation Order with a condition of treatment (Powers of Criminal Courts Act 1973). The former, Guardianship, is the most interesting if least used (Mental Health Act Commission 1997). It is interesting because Guardianship under the 1959 Act, as recommended by the Percy Commission (1957), was to provide compulsory care for patients outside the mental hospital who could not be persuaded to accept help or training on a voluntary basis. In other words, Guardianship was a de facto Community Treatment Order, with many of its powers. The Percy Commission suggested that Guardianship might be more appropriate for those with mild or chronic forms of mental illness (that is, not acute), and hoped that as community psychiatric services developed Guardianship would become more popular.

This hope has not been borne out, although recently there has been a slight increase in its use. There were 434 new cases in England during the year ending 31 March 1998, representing a 6% increase on 1997 and almost double that of 1992 (Mental Health Act Commission 1999). Whether this represents a change of heart is difficult to say; at this stage, it may be safer to assume that no clear trend has emerged. However, without that earlier decline we might not have needed the community order or the Supervision Register in the first place. In spite of the Percy Commission, Guardianship has been used predominantly for the mentally impaired and the severely mentally impaired (ibid. 1999; Department of Health/Home Office 1978, paras 4.6 and 4.7).

In 1978, in an attempt to reverse the existing trend, the Department of Health considered Guardianship under the 1959 Act. It suggested that the extensive nature of the Guardian's powers, and all that was involved in exercising them, was a major factor in its decline (ibid. 1978, para. 4.8). The Guardian had the powers of a father over a child aged

14 (the patient must be at least 16 years old) and it was thought that local authorities were reluctant to take on these responsibilities. Accordingly, under the 1983 Act, powers were reduced, so that the Guardian was no longer given the power to impose treatment. This became the so-called 'essential powers' approach and was the preferred option. This gave the Guardian the power:

(a)   to require the patient to reside at a place specified by the Guardian or the local social services authority,
(b)   to require the patient to attend at places and times similarly specified for the purpose of medical treatment, occupation, education or training, and
(c)   to require access to the patient to be given, at any place where the patient is residing, to any doctor, approved social worker, or other person similarly specified. (Sections 8(2) and 40(2))

A Guardianship Order lasts for six months initially but may be renewed for a further six months, and then for a year at a time (Section 20(1)). The Guardian is usually a local authority social worker. Under this 'essential powers' approach, there is no power to impose treatment – (b) above requires the patient to attend for treatment but there is no power to enforce it, nor is there any right to recall the patient to a mental hospital. Paradoxically, these restrictions have added to a further loss of confidence in Guardianship: initially its powers were seen as too severe, so these were modified under the 1983 Act, but by then the climate had changed and more controls were being asked for.

In spite of a recent increase in use, Guardianship is now discussed so rarely that, to all intents and purposes, it is no longer a serious feature in the community control debate. The Mental Health Act Commission rarely mention it in their biennial reports, this in spite of the hope by Brenda Hoggett (1984) that the 'essential powers' approach might encourage local authorities to take on more Guardianship Orders. She also believed that the 'essential powers' approach gave the mentally disordered patient more rights (such as the right to refuse treatment), as a Guardianship Order under the 1959 Act represented that old-style paternalism which under the guise of benevolence allowed rights to be removed (Hoggett 1984, p. 307). Unfortunately, Brenda Hoggett's hopes for a revitalised Guardianship Order have not been realised; although they may if the current improvement continues. Community safety stresses the rights of the community to be protected against the mentally disordered. Controlling the mentally disordered is what the modern approach is about.

Probation Orders with a condition of treatment share a similar fate. They too involve supervision by an outside agency – in this case the probation officer as opposed to local authority social workers – and, as with Guardianship, those patients on a Probation Order have the right to refuse treatment. Briefly, the Powers of the Criminal Courts Act 1973 permits the court to attach a condition of treatment to a Probation Order, which may be as an inpatient or outpatient, if the court is satisfied, on the evidence of a duly qualified medical practitioner, that the offender's mental condition is such that it requires and may be susceptible to treatment, but is not such as to warrant detention in hospital under the Mental Health Act 1983. This apparent confusion turns out to be resolved thus: a person on a Probation Order with a condition of treatment can be detained in a hospital but, unlike those patients detained under the Mental Health Act 1983, his condition will not be as severe, and while on probation he has the same rights while in hospital as an outpatient to refuse treatment and discharge himself. That, of course, may lead to a breach of probation, but if a refusal to undergo treatment is reasonable, having regard to all the circumstances (Section 6(7) of the Powers of Criminal Courts Act 1973), no breach would be implied. Tim Exworthy says the main advantages of psychiatric Probation Orders is that they can be employed in cases not warranting detention under the Mental Health Act 1983, and are able to provide treatment in conditions falling outside the 1983 Act definitions of mental disorder, for example sexual deviance and alcohol and drug misuse (Exworthy 1995).

There seems to be general agreement that what is commonly called the psychiatric Probation Order – or more accurately a Probation Order with a condition of psychiatric treatment as essentially determined by Section 3 of the Powers of Criminal Courts Act 1973 – is underused, undervalued and underresearched. As far as can be seen, the high point of the order was in the mid 1970s, when approximately 1,000 outpatient and 500 inpatient orders were made – 'approximately' because, surprisingly, there were few accurate national statistics on the orders made. By 1987, the figures had dipped to 870 and 150 respectively and by the late 1990s they had dropped even further.

It is difficult to explain the lack of interest. It may have something to do with a general reluctance on behalf of psychiatrists to accept patients on an order, and a similar reluctance by the probation service to negotiate with psychiatrists about resolving existing tensions. (The most obvious are caused by a lack of cooperation between the probation service and psychiatrists, where there were calls for greater cooperation between the agencies to improve their effectiveness.) The courts also seem to have lost interest, or perhaps have simply gone along with the prevailing climate. No one seems to know. Only one detailed research study has been undertaken, and that as far back as 1980 (Lewis 1980). This study looked at the use and effectiveness of such orders. The conclusions were generally favourable, with Lewis arguing for greater use, especially among the less severely mentally disordered. Sadly, the study produced little general interest and has hardly been referred to again.

The 1991 Criminal Justice Act attempted to revive things by placing community treatments at the centre of the criminal justice system. Section 9 allowed the court to require the offender to comply, during the whole or part of the period on probation, with such requirements as the court considered desirable, while Section 4 requires the court 'where an offender appears to be mentally disordered, to obtain and consider a medical report before passing a custodial sentence other than one fixed by law'. The 1991 Act seems not to have improved things, with the decline continuing. It is difficult to know how that decline can be reversed.

Finally, extended leave under Section 17 of the Mental Health Act 1983; this section provides leave of absence for those patients subject to detention under Sections 3 and 37 of the 1983 Act. It can be given at the discretion of the Responsible Medical Officer (RMO) – there is no authority under the Act for the RMO, the psychiatrist in charge, to delegate powers to other hospital staff, although the RMO may instruct nursing staff not to implement authorised leave on medical grounds at their discretion. The length of leave must not exceed the duration of the current detaining order, and the order can only be renewed if the patient is in hospital. The provisions of Section 17 apply without modification to all patients subject to Hospital and Guardianship Orders; they also apply to restricted patients where the approval of the Home Secretary is required.

The MHAC noted that there is considerable misunderstanding over the requirements of Section 17 (Mental Health Act Commission 1995, para. 9.4). It said that many still believe, incorrectly, that a detained patient may go on leave without completion of Section 17 formalities, if they are only going out of the hospital grounds for a short while, or if escorted by staff. The Commission gives examples of what it calls bad practice where nursing staff have withheld leave because a patient would not attend ward meetings; the Commission says that deterioration in the patient's mental state is the only justification for withholding leave. Other examples of bad practice include the use of Section 17 to move a patient from a district hospital with severe management problems to a regional secure unit or simply from one hospital to another. In the first, the move invariably takes place during an acute phase of mental disorder, and removes the patient from easy access to his RMO – transfer would be more appropriate.

It was a similar abuse of Section 17 that led to the famous cases of *Hallstrom* and *Gardiner* in 1986, which led directly to the Mental Health (Patients in the Community) Act 1995. Briefly, a practice had developed whereby patients on Section 17 had been granted home leave, and were recalled to hospital for a few days or perhaps for one night, in order to renew the order. Psychiatrists used this period of leave and the subsequent recall to produce a de facto Community Treatment Order. This practice was somewhat distastefully described as the 'long leash' procedure. The landmark judgements of *Regina* v. *Hallstrom and Another ex parte W* and *Regina* v. *Gardiner and Another ex parte L* pronounced these practices as unlawful (Bean and Mounser 1993). The High Court said that 'to recall was to extend the duration of the liability to recall' and that to do so was unlawful for, among other things, 'it was a way by which psychiatrists took preventative action in anticipation of a potential relapse' (quoted in Exworthy 1995, p. 220).

Other provisions for providing care in the community involve Conditionally Discharged Restricted Patients (under Section 41 of the 1983 Act) which usually carry the requirements of regular psychiatric and social supervision, thus enabling statutory aftercare to be provided. While subject to restrictions in the community, the patient remains liable to be recalled to hospital if at any time there is failure to comply with supervision, or the patient's behaviour gives cause for concern, or the psychiatric condition deteriorates (ibid. p. 222). The Criminal Procedure (Insanity and Unfitness to Plead) Act 1991 established a new provision for providing care in the community. It applies only to a small group of patients found unfit to plead at their trial who can be made subject to a supervision and treatment order, if the court is satisfied, on the evidence of the doctors, that the person's mental condition is not serious enough to require a Hospital Order or a Guardianship Order. The defendant has to submit to treatment, which may not exceed two years, but if the defendant then becomes fit to plead, the trial can take place. These last two provisions need not concern us greatly: they involve small numbers of patients and remain marginal to the main concerns – important though they may be for those patients under those orders.

The nature of Supervision Orders and community surveillance

Briefly, the purpose of Supervision Registers, according to the Health Service Guidelines HSC(94)5 (Department of Health 1994), is to identify all patients under the care of a NHS provider unit known to be at significant risk, or potentially at significant risk, of committing serious violence or suicide, or of serious neglect as a result of severe and enduring mental illness. They are seen as a key element in the government strategy aimed at:

(a) providing a care plan that aims to reduce the risk and ensure that the patient's care needs are reviewed regularly and that contact by a key worker is maintained;

(b) providing a point of reference for relevant and authorised health and social services staff to enquire whether individuals under the Care Programme are at risk;

(c) planning for the facilities and resources necessary to meet the needs of this group of patients, and

(d) identifying those patients who should receive the highest priority for care and active follow-up.

Patients suffering from mental illness in this context include those with personality and psychopathic disorders who are receiving treatment from specialist psychiatric services.

The Care Programme Approach (or CPA) in (b) above was introduced in 1991 as the cornerstone of government mental health policy (Department of Health 1990). It is designed to improve the coordination of care for people with severe mental health needs, and applies to all who are referred and accepted by specialist mental health services, over the age of 16 years. Patients placed on the Supervision Register will have had a CPA review and been allocated a key worker, that is, someone who *inter alia* ensures that a needs assessment exercise is completed at the early stages of contact, alongside a risk assessment which includes the views and opinions of other members of the multidisciplinary team involved in the treatment. The decision to include a person on the Register is made by the consultant psychiatrist responsible for that person's care, and there is no right of appeal. Not all patients will know they are on the Register, 'as some who for clinical reasons will not be informed, if to do so would probably cause serious harm to his or her physical health' (Department of Health 1994, GGL(94)5, Annex A, para. 12). The Guidelines say that patients on the Register should be reviewed regularly, at least every six months, and the patient should be withdrawn from the Register if he or she is no longer considered a serious risk. Entry on the Register should be confidential, as with other health records, although information from the Register should be accessible to other mental health professionals on a 'need to know' basis, in order to plan or provide care.

This brief overview highlights some of the central features of Supervision Registers. How effective are they? With little or no research, it is a difficult question to answer, but a trawl of the literature suggests that they have few supporters outside the Department of Health. Most of the criticisms are of the legal rights variety, such as there is no independent review of the decision to put someone on a Supervision Register, and no mechanism for appeal by an included person (Harrison 1994, p. 1017). Caldicott states that:

Anxieties in relation to civil liberties and the registers remain. Concern has also been expressed about the possible implications for the patient of having his/her name included on such a register. (1994, p. 386)

Estella Baker has provided the most trenchant criticisms, arguing that the Registers have little genuine merit in terms of public safety, and that the decision to include patients on them 'are so arbitrary as to be contrary to human rights' (Baker 1997, p. 32).

Let us consider the question of confidentiality in the light of the following hypothetical case. A policeman is called to a house to deal with a domestic violence incident at 23.00 on Friday evening. He suspects that the male offender is mentally ill and may be receiving psychiatric care. However, after a short time, he believes that the situation has calmed down and he leaves, with a suggestion that the offender sees his GP as soon as possible. The police officer calls the Supervision Register office to check if the offender is on the Register. He is in fact and is regarded as a very serious risk to women. The Register office, however, is manned by a night duty clerk with no access to the Register and he informs the constable that, even if he had access, he could not give the details to the police. In the early hours of Saturday morning the offender kills his partner.

What then? Who is to blame? Can the police be criticised, or is it the fault of the NHS provider unit? Above all, if the Register cannot help in a case such as this, what use is it? The Guidelines say that disclosure to other agencies (they list probation and 'other criminal justice agencies' but do not include the police) may be either if the patient consents, or without consent if disclosure can be justified in the public interest. The provider unit must be able to justify such disclosures, taking full account of the view of the consultant psychiatrist responsible for the care of the patient (para. 21). It is rare for the police to be given access.

The provider unit may also bring the case to the newly formed Public Protection Panels, who could decide to provide surveillance or some other programme for the patient. These would be the exceptions, otherwise the police would not be involved.

To the question asked above, 'what use is the Register?', the answer is difficult. The official version is that the Registers form part of the CPA, a policy concerned with those patients most at risk to themselves or others who should receive adequate care, support and supervision in the community to assist in preventing them from falling through the care network. The *Health of the Nation* White Paper (Department of Health 1992a) stressed the requirement to develop information systems designed to ensure that patients at risk of relapse did not get lost to follow-up, and a so-called alert status be used to designate individuals at particular risk to themselves or to others. The Supervision Register is said to be a logical extension of this proposal and now supersedes it. Then there is the Ten Point Plan announced by the Secretary of State in August 1993 to improve community care for mentally ill people. It contained a commitment to introduce special Supervision Registers for patients who are most at risk and need most support, as part of the development of mental health information systems generally (Department of Health 1994, Annex A, paras 1(a), (b) and (c)). This official version does not of itself answer the question about effectiveness, all it does is put the Register in the context of government policy. Without detailed research, the question about effectiveness cannot be answered, although the Department of Health is more confident, seeing them as capable of protecting the vulnerable patients and the wider public.

These comments from the Department of Health have to be set against a series of other trenchant criticisms, not least from the MHAC (Mental Health Act Commission 1995, para. 10.3) who report on the way 'token' Supervision Orders have been produced in some hospitals but not fully implemented. In others, there are problems of interpretation in relation to the inclusion on the Register, to informing the patient of inclusion and access to the Register being 'areas in which Commission members have noted a wide variation in practice' (ibid. p. 133). The MHAC gave the example where inclusion on one Register was on the basis that the patient was thought to have committed a crime, on another the local police *were* informed of everybody placed on the Register – this being an unusual occurrence. The Commission also noted some of the problems concerning the way ASWs related to the Register. Ever the optimist, the Commission expected those difficulties would soon be resolved.

Nor is it easy to escape the obvious civil rights questions that such Registers produce and highlighted by Estella Baker. The inclusion criteria are unclear, broad and ambiguous, as are the termination criteria – 'the registered person should be withdrawn from the Register if he/she is no longer considered to be at significant risk' – it being much more difficult to show that someone is no longer at risk than being at risk in the first place. There are numerous civil rights questions, such as the way a database operates, for example keeping some patients on the database because they are on the database – a tautological justification but not uncommon with databases of this nature. That not all patients know they are on the Register is really quite scandalous, and likely to have a long-term impact on the way mentally disordered patients are perceived.

To the question, was a Register needed?, the answer is, almost certainly not. If, as was sometimes claimed, it was to target resources to a group of patients with high visible needs, then the Register clearly fails. If the Register is to assist what Tim Exworthy suggests is to be a community care programme which must be assertive, proactive and pursued vigorously and wholeheartedly (Exworthy 1995, p. 237), then again the Register may not be achieving this. Making contact with hard to reach violent patients is not likely to occur as a result of a Register; this requires skilled outreach workers rather than a list of patients at risk. In Exworthy's terms, 'improvements in prevention of serious harm are then unlikely' and 'legal measures do not cover up or correct financial inadequacies, if anything they expose them more starkly' (ibid. p. 237). Moreover, introducing the Register by way of a set of Guidelines rather than full-scale legislation was 'legislating by the back door' – MIND went so far as to argue that the Department of Health acted *ultra vires* in using the Guidelines to require health authorities to introduce the Register (ibid. p. 237). Not surprisingly, the Department of Health rejects such criticism. Whether so or not, experience with other Registers suggests that they consume vast amounts of resources without doing much to reduce risk. We already have Public Protection Panels, Supervision Registers merely add another block to an ever-growing control system. They have now been withdrawn, but provide an example of how controls were introduced hurriedly and without thought for the future.

The main interest here is in those patients subject to a Community Treatment Order, also known as a Community Supervision Order, a Community Care Order, and a Supervised Discharge Order – the terms can be used interchangeably and characterise the debate about supervision in the community. Not included is preventative commitment, sometimes called supervised treatment, which is common to the

USA, and which allows patients to be placed on supervised treatment irrespective of whether they are hospital inpatients. Supervised treatment takes us into different territory.

Community Supervision Orders are slightly different, but they too are open to vigorous criticisms. It is equally doubtful if they were needed, the more so according to the recent figures on their use. These orders came into operation on 1 April 1996; they are also part of the Ten Point Plan. They apply to non-restricted patients who have been detained in hospital under the Mental Health Act 1983 under Sections 3, 37, 47 or 48, and who present a serious risk to their health or safety, or to the safety of other people unless their aftercare was supervised. To emphasise the point; community discharge differs from preventative commitment, for the former applies only to patients who are detained in hospital, that is, as aftercare, while a Preventative Commitment Order can apply to any patient, whether in hospital or not.

The MHAC says the purpose of Supervised Discharge is to help to ensure that patients who have been detained for treatment receive aftercare services provided under Section 117 (Mental Health Act Commission 1999). The patient must present a substantial risk of serious harm to his health or safety or the safety of others or of being exploited. In spite of all the protests, all the debates and all the expectations from government, it turns out that there are few applications made. There were 318 in England in 1997/98 and 11 in Wales which, although this was 50% more than the previous year, still falls far short of the 3,000 patients estimated by the Department of Health in 1993 as likely to be suitable for this new power.

The MHAC believes that one obstacle is the cumbersome and bureaucratic application procedures. The power is also perceived as ineffective, in that treatment cannot be enforced and there are practical difficulties in exercising the powers that do exist (Mental Health Act Commission 1999, para. 4.121, p. 111). Inevitably, there are wide variations in use depending on local policy and practice (ibid. p. 112) but, with little or no research, what is one to make of that? The MHAC sees Supervised Discharge as of value to those patients needing control and direction during their period of discharge but can say little more.

However, Nigel Eastman (1997) is deeply sceptical. He says a legal power over patients is merely one clinical tool, to be judged in its efficacy as such, and adds that it is not the proper role of a doctor to campaign for particular powers or their absence. He quotes with approval the Registrar of the Royal College of Psychiatrists, who say the Mental Health (Patients in the Community) Act 1995 which was legally effective on the 1 April 1996 represents:

> the worst of all possible worlds. The mentally ill will be subject to the power of 'arrest' and to no apparent purpose... The act will not provide the extra public safety which the Government is hoping for. (quoted in ibid. 1997, p. 495)

There is probably little that can be done to change the way governments appear to insist that solutions to the problems of the mentally disordered in the community can be sought through an increase in the nature and extent of controls. The government *Review of the Mental Health Act 1983* (Department of Health 1999) had as its terms of reference a legislative framework that included compulsory treatment in the community.

> Ministers made it quite clear that, for a small number of these patients for reason of either a risk to their own safety and health of others, compliance with agreed treatment plans should not be optional. (para. 2)

Accordingly the Committee came up with a proposal for a Compulsory Order which would apply to patients living inside and outside hospital (para. 103) and it would be up to the clinical supervisor to specify within the care and treatment plan the appropriate location and the reasons for it (para. 105). The conditions would not be dissimilar from those under the civil powers of the existing 1983 Act.

This proposal may receive much sympathy from the government, but it has within it a set of assumptions, one of which is to equate the community with the hospital as if they offer similar therapeutic opportunities. Yet control over patients in the community is quite different from control over patients in a hospital, the latter is an enclosed institution geared up to providing treatment, the former is not. Consider how the patient is to receive medication. Compulsory medication in hospital may involve all the features of medication in the community – which may incidentally involve considerable force – but it is not public, and it is given in front of a limited audience. In the community it *is* public and may be in front of an unsympathetic audience. What public treatment does to the doctor–patient relationship is something else again. I fear that community treatment pushes us more and more into shark-infested waters where nearly all those involved, patients and treatment agents alike, will come out rather badly mauled.

A brief overview and discussion of community safety and control

Tim Exworthy argues that the ethos of care in the community includes prevention; this in contrast to Compulsory Orders to hospital which ensure supervision, treatment and compliance with that treatment (Exworthy 1995, p. 223). But preventing what? Presumably preventing psychiatric relapses, but also preventing an increase in social emergencies, and by definition actively promoting community safety. Consider a case example taken from an earlier research study (Bean 1980). 'Here is a woman in her late 30s with two young children, who is a single parent. She is no longer taking her medication. She had a spell in hospital earlier and was discharged with a diagnosis of schizophrenia in remission. The early symptoms were returning and she had to be compulsorily readmitted and the children were taken into care.' Had she been on a Compulsory Supervision Order, she probably would have taken her medication, avoided another period in hospital and the children need not have been taken into care. Supervision could be expected to produce treatment and the prevention of further disruption.

Leaving aside for the moment whether supervision should or can produce the desired effects, what are some of the implications of this movement towards community care and controls? As far as the recent history is concerned, there were three important stages; first, the proposals submitted by the British Association of Social Work (BASW), second, the legal judgements of *Hallstrom* and *Gardiner*, and finally, the proposals from the Royal College of Psychiatrists. In the first, BASW (1977) proposed that a Community Care Order should be introduced 'to meet our aspirations to care for patients in the least restrictive conditions possible within their own living environment'. This Community Care Order would provide compulsory powers to provide care within the community for use 'when the individual refuses or is unable to agree with the recommendation he is in need of care' (quoted in Bean and Mounser 1994). That some critics sardonically pointed out that the social services departments already had a Community Treatment Order, it was called Guardianship and rarely used (then only about 50 per year), seemed not to matter. However, BASW's proposals might have gone no further but for the decisions by the High Court in *Regina* v. *Hallstrom and Another ex parte W* and *Regina* v. *Gardiner and Another ex parte L*, where the so-called 'long leash' activities were adjudged unlawful. This led the Royal College of Psychiatrists to produce two discussion documents, in April and October 1987, which provided the main thrust to the debate, and greatly influenced Parliament in the final outcome (Royal College of Psychiatrists 1987).

These discussion documents produced the first salvo in what has become a long-running battle between two opposing camps. The supporting group consisted, and still consists, largely of organisations representing patients' families, alongside those concerned with community safety. They see the merits of supervision, and welcome an increase in controls. They argue that the patient's freedom of choice is not restricted by community controls: freedom of choice being already restricted by the patient's mental condition. The aims and justifications for controls are to provide treatment, albeit through enforced treatment which restores the patient's choices and hence the patient's freedoms. At first this includes freedom from symptoms, but later produces freedoms at a higher level than hitherto. Community controls provide the least restrictive form of care consistent with safe management.

On the other side are disparate groups of individuals mainly concerned with patients' civil rights. They fear that a dangerous precedent has been created by a growing increase in community controls – proposals for the Community Care Order, with its absence of judicial controls, were the main object of their dislike. These groups emphasise civil rights and do so through a reductionist approach to the care of the mentally disordered, which means they begin by adopting a sceptical position demanding that the onus is on those wishing to increase controls to make their justifications clear. They saw proposals for a Community Care Order as but the thin end of an increasingly large wedge, where more and more controls were being heaped on more and more patients. Support for this side of the debate comes from organisations such as MIND and, surprisingly, the MHAC, who said in 1993 that it was unable to support the Royal College's proposals in the form in which they were put and offered counter proposals. The Commission thought that there was scope in the 1983 Act for greater use of Guardianship, and for extended use of the leave from hospital procedures (Mental Health Act Commission 1993, para. 12.5).

These battle lines have reappeared. Community safety comes into the debate on the side of those supporting community controls. It is primarily an interventionist strategy. Those wanting increasing amounts of control (and they would say if that includes more treatment, then so much the better) justify their position because they believe mental disorder reduces or renders patients unable to control themselves. Critics quickly point out that community safety is a 'net widening' activity, that is, it creates more and more rules which bring more and more people into the criminal justice system, or in this case, brings more and more into the mental health system. The dichotomy is neatly summarised thus: 'Some people are deprived of their liberties in an attempt to give them psychiatric care. Occasionally others are deprived of psychiatric care in an attempt to guard their liberties' (quoted in Exworthy 1995, p. 218).

At present there is little doubt that the community safety lobby (positive libertarians) is ascendant. One searches in vain for any government statement that gives hope for the opposing reductionist groups; in contrast, the community safety view is often put, and rarely challenged. Looking through the Expert Committee Report on the 1983 Act (Department of Health 1999), reference is often made to the civil rights of the patients – civil rights in this context means a negative libertarian argument – but not a great deal is done to enlarge them, or create new ones. It is almost as if the Committee were told of the government's wishes to continue with and perhaps expand community controls and were expected to frame their Report accordingly. They have provided few objections to the principles underlying the Community Treatment Orders, with the result that it appears as if we have to accept the inevitability of more community controls.

Placing community controls in a wider context, it is not difficult to see how the demand for community supervision grew out of the failings of community care, or, more specifically, from the failings of that small but not insignificant number of persons who were not given adequate support to live independently in the community, or how, after one or two dramatic fatalities, followed by the growth of highly vocal pressure groups, the government had to show it was acting in the public interest and doing something about the problem. One could see the solution in slightly different, more sardonic terms perhaps: that the government had to find a way in which it appeared to act decisively, but in effect was doing little except avoiding giving more resources to community care. So, for example, Exworthy, in his interesting review of community provisions, lists a number of critics who point to the absurdity of providing crisis orientated care for disorders that run chronic courses. These critics were no more enthusiastic about a Community Treatment Order than others, seeing it as producing what they called 'episodic rather than continuous care', or as an inappropriate response which provides treatment only when symptoms are evident (Exworthy 1995, pp. 223–4). The government, however, claims that community supervision provides continuity of care but Coid warns that:

> taking up these recommendations without simultaneously addressing
> resources has introduced a mechanism which allocates responsibility

and identifies the recipient for blame for failures in the future
but diverts attention away from the resources issue. (quoted in ibid.
p. 238)

The Community Care Order fits into that general scheme of things,
including the social and political climate of the times, where toughness,
surveillance and increasing controls are the watchword. Experiences
from the criminal justice system are salutary; they show that community
supervision becomes part of a wider trend away from the focused
characteristics of therapy towards a system of vigorously enforced
intermediate punishments aimed at serving better the victims (patients)
and the community together. Community supervision is but one step in
this direction. It is roughly equivalent to the Probation Order, at least
the later version, for the earlier Probation Order has been overtaken
by demands for stricter punishments where the goal is toughness
in appearance if nothing else. Community supervision is less about
providing help, more about controls, as is the new version of the Probation Order. Already, the mental health services are beginning to follow
the criminal justice system, where demands for a even stricter Community Care Order have been made, positioning them somewhere
between the existing Community Care Order and the rigours of the
old-style mental hospital. Proposals for changing the 1983 Act are also
for a stricter, tougher Community Care Order.

One can see parallels with the Probation Order in other ways.
Changes in the criminal justice system began in the mid 1980s, as a
result of a sense of disillusionment with existing probation practices
alongside an increasing level of fear of crime – what Mulvey et al. call
'networks of benevolent coercion that have degenerated into vehicles
for social monitoring but carry little rehabilitative effect' (quoted in
ibid. p. 225). These practices were using valuable resources, but also
claiming to be expanding their effectiveness. In practice, they were
'doing more of what they were doing before, but not necessarily
differently' (ibid.). The overall effect was to widen the net of legal
compulsion without delivering more effective care.

Running alongside this critique of probation was a second critique,
articulated by Norval Morris and Michael Tonry in their influential
book *Between Prison and Probation* (1990), which was concerned with
reducing the prison population in the USA. They said judges were
faced with a polarised choice between prison and probation, with little
or nothing in between. Prison was too hard and probation too soft, yet
the decision to send the offender to one rather than the other was
paper thin. What was needed, Morris and Tonry said, was a series of

intermediate sanctions capable of filling that vacuum, a set of mid-range punishments:

> The justice system needs an alternative, intermediate form of punishment for these offenders who are too anti social for the relative freedom that probation now offers, but not so seriously criminal as to require imprisonment. A sanction is needed that would impose intensive surveillance, coupled with substantial community services and restriction. (Morris and Tonry, quoted in Petersilia 1998, p. 4)

Accordingly, intensive probation programmes were developed, first in the USA and later in Britain. They were aimed at diverting low-risk prisoners to the community, that is, taking them out of the prison system, or diverting high-risk probationers to smaller case loads with more intensive controls. Joan Petersilia adds that, as the cold war wound down, the defence industry, along with the developing computer and electronics industries, saw the community correction clientele as a growing market. Electronic monitoring, on-site drug testing, voice verification systems and so on allowed community corrections to become more community orientated, using the offender's home as a place of incarceration (Petersilia 1998, p. 5). She adds 'Jurisdictions could choose from a menu of bells and whistles which include surveillance and services, and the goal came to be toughness in appearance' (ibid. p. 5).

The effect has been to develop and promote that midway area between prison and probation in a manner which integrates surveillance with treatment. (Even boot camps are shifting from a reliance on physical militaristic planning towards therapeutic goals, illustrating that today's theme is a mixture of coercion and therapy whatever the setting: see ibid. p. 7.) Jointly run programmes, according to Petersilia, reinforce the legacy of a decade of experimentation, as no single agency can be expected to reduce crime (ibid. p. 9). So too, presumably, with mental health; one can almost hear the same arguments being advanced – that future developments will not be found where treatment is provided as of choice, nor on the back of a modest degree of surveillance. Mental health, or at least community mental health, like crime, is a complex multifaceted problem that will not be overcome by simplistic, singularly focused solutions. Workable long-term solutions must come from joint agency ventures which involve the community and are embraced and actively supported there. Where the message is taken from the criminal justice system, it will be that community programmes need to be developed to fill the gap between hospital and outpatient clinics, with increased measures of surveillance – low-level surveillance will not be acceptable. They need also to move towards joint agency operations, and involve community programmes alongside others which are more coercive. The Community Care Order becomes but one step in this movement, so that mental health unwittingly gets pushed closer to criminal justice. That would seem to be the future; whether it is the future that is best for mental health is another matter.

The problem is that while there are some lessons to be learned from the criminal justice system, the two systems are widely different in aims and objectives. Intensive probation was aimed at keeping offenders out of prison, because traditional probation, being too lax, encouraged probation officers to introduce 'breach' proceedings where stricter controls might have prevented that. In mental health the same considerations may appear to apply, at least on the surface (that is, community treatments stop patients entering mental hospitals), but the difference is in the nature of the sanctions. Prisons are rightly used as sanctions for those breaking the Probation Order; do we really want to see the mental hospital in a similar position? How can such a view be reconciled with the message that has been put over by psychiatry for decades that 'mental illness is an illness like any other and the mental hospital is a hospital like any other'? Are we now to see it as a place of punishment? Moreover, there are entirely adequate provisions for dealing with the mentally disordered under various sections of the Mental Health Act. Are these to be supplanted, or perhaps supplemented by new provisions? As yet, no satisfactory answers to these questions have appeared.

Conclusion

Controls represent a triumph of that wing of the public safety lobby, which begins with the assumption that greater levels of public safety can be achieved through Registers and community supervision. The evidence for this has never been forthcoming; Registers and community supervision involve a leap of blind faith against which have to be set the loss of civil liberties for the patient and little genuine merit for the rest of us.

One could have more sympathy with that view of public safety had the government of the day sought to introduce Registers and supervision with due respect for civil rights, not just for the public generally but for the patient and all concerned. Supervision Registers were introduced by the back door as it were by Circular HSG(94)5 (Department of Health 1994), that is, not through full-scale legislation, and the Community Supervision Order was introduced with no right of appeal prior to the order being made – although there is a possibility of appeal to a MHRT afterwards – and with little regard for the rights of those under supervision. Perhaps we should be glad it is used so infrequently, although that does not reduce the point that patients on the order have little opportunity to seek redress. Estella Baker again:

> In so far as pursuit of the community care programme did influence the content of the proposal (for Supervision Registers) the uppermost concern seems to have been to address the need to regulate the delivery of psychiatric care in the post hospital era rather than protect patients from the risks of violence and neglect. (ibid. p. 32)

It is not so much that the battle has been lost, but that there are more battles ahead. One can see what will happen. In a few years time, there will be complaints that the existing system is not tight enough and allows certain types of patient who are considered dangerous to slip through the net. The demand will be for new controls for this group. Then a few years later another group of dangerous patients will be identified as also slipping through the net, so additional controls will be wanted for this group, and so on and so on. The psychiatrist Peter Scott said, when discussing the introduction of regional secure units in 1970, that these were not the solution. There would be more and more demands for more and more units to take more and more patients, all on the grounds that existing laws needed to be refined to take those patients that were slipping through the existing net (Scott 1970). So too with the Supervision Register. Demands will be made to make it more efficient, that is, to put more patients on a different type of Register, keep them on for a longer period and allow more agencies access to the data. Sadly, this is the way control systems work; they have an enormous capacity to enlarge themselves and have many supporters who want to see them enlarged. My personal view is that we should treat demands for enlargement with scepticism, and insist that all controls, new or otherwise, have adequate protection for patients and others alike.

5

Policing the Mentally Disordered

The civil commitment procedures under Sections 2, 3 and 4 of the 1983 Mental Health Act give powers for patients to be detained in hospitals when the patients are seen and examined in their own homes. Powers exist under Section 136 of the Act for patients in a public place, if they appear to be suffering from mental disorder, to be taken to a place of safety where they can be seen by a psychiatrist and an ASW in order that a decision can be made about treatment and care. Briefly, the legislation authorises a

police constable who finds a person who appears to be suffering from mental disorder in a place to which the public have access to remove that person to a place of safety. He may do so, if the person

(a) Appears to be in immediate need of care and control
(b) If the constable thinks it is necessary to do so in the interests of that person or for the protection of other persons.

A person so removed to a place of safety may be detained for a period not exceeding 72 hours.

A place of safety can include a police station, a hospital, mental nursing home, residential accommodation or other suitable place, the owner of which is willing to receive the patient. There is no right of appeal against the order.

Section 135 of the 1983 Act authorises a police constable, on an order issued by a magistrate, to enter a home, by force if necessary, of a person believed to be suffering from mental disorder, and remove that person with a view to detaining him, under another section of the Act, in a place of safety. The police officer must be accompanied by an ASW and a medical practitioner. The information must be provided on oath – the initiative is likely to come from an ASW. The information must state that it appears there are reasonable grounds to suspect that the person is believed to be suffering from mental disorder and,

(a) Has been, or is being, ill treated, neglected or kept otherwise than under proper control, or,
(b) Is a person unable to care for himself and is living alone.

The Justice may, if satisfied, issue a warrant, but the patient shall not be named in any information or warrant. A patient may be detained under this section for a period not exceeding 72 hours.

Other sections of the 1983 Act which involve the police are Section 18(3) where there is power to arrest mentally disordered persons who have absented themselves from a hospital without leave or failed to return from leave. Section 38(7) gives a constable power to arrest any mentally disordered person detained under a Hospital Order. Under Section 137(2) a police officer, when he takes a person into custody, and conveys or detains him, has 'all the powers, authorities, protection and privileges which a constable has within the area for which he acts as constable'. Under Section 136, the patient taken to the police station is arrested. That means *inter alia* that:

(a) the patients have a right to an Appropriate Adult (see Chapter 6) and,
(b) the patients can be searched under Section 32 of the PACE (1984) which says:

A constable may search an arrested person in any case where a person to be searched has been arrested at a place other than a police station if the constable has reasonable grounds for believing that the arrested person may present a danger to himself or others.

The power to search is a continuing one and may be used at any time while the person is detained at a police station.

Unfortunately there are no central records showing the numbers of patients detained under Sections 136 or 135; Bluglass (1983) gave a rough estimate for 1979 when he said:

there were 1623 persons removed to a hospital as a place of safety, and Section 135 was used on an average of 9 occasions annually in England and Wales since 1974. (p. 134)

Other commentators give similar figures for later years but they too are estimates. Many police forces detain patients, ostensibly under Section 136, but without recording it as such, so that the full extent of use is not known, although it is believed that there is an increase in its use over the country as a whole.

The key features of Section 136 have been examined elsewhere (Bean 1999), including the duties of those undertaking the assessment, some aspects of the legal terminology (for example what constitutes a 'place of safety' or a 'public place') and questions about how many 'places of safety' can be used for each patient. The aim here is highlight some additional features, linking them to matters of community safety and the integrity of the mental health services. A separate discussion in the second part of the chapter concerns the use of FMEs within the police station; this is not directly related to Section 136, but includes police practices and the way the mentally disordered are processed. It needs to be stressed, yet again, that the research evidence is limited – only four studies have been undertaken on Section 136 (see ibid.) and none on Section 135.

Detaining patients

Section 136 gives police the power to detain non-criminal patients and take them to a place of safety, which can be and often is a police station. Many commentators regard this as an anomaly; they dislike the idea of the police station being used to detain the mentally disordered. The use of a police station is said to be unsuitable mainly because it criminalises mental disorder. Moreover, critics say, the police are not trained in the diagnosis of mental disorder, yet Section 136 requires them to say that 'it appears to them the person is mentally disordered', that is, the police are required to give a low-level diagnosis. Nor, it is said, are they trained in managing a mentally disordered person when he is detained in a place of safety; the criticism then extends beyond the use of the police station to the police themselves.

Leaving aside those questions for the moment, it seems axiomatic that a policy of community care will push the police into a more central role in dealing with the mentally disordered. Mental patients who create disturbances in a public place come to the notice of the police, and, because all psychiatric emergencies are social emergencies, police involvement is to be expected. Moreover, were Section 136 to be repealed, it is highly likely that the police would act as before, except that without Section 136 they would arrest the patient and charge him, probably under a public order offence, rather than detain him under the Mental Health Act as at present. Paradoxically, that would lead to additional criminalisation. Moreover, as things now stand, where a mentally disordered person is charged with an offence, the charge may be set aside if it is in the public interest to do so (Home Office 1990, para. 4), in which case the police can detain the patient under Section 136.

The second point is more of a question than a statement. Assume that it is not in the interests of the police to be involved in Section 136, then who else is there? The simple answer is, there is no one. It is unlikely that another occupational group would or could provide a 24-hour, 365 day per year service, or be prepared to take on, or have the facilities to deal with, mentally disordered patients, some of whom may be violent, and all of whom pose problems. Community psychiatric nurses (CPNs) or social workers would be possible contenders, but CPNs have never expressed any willingness to be so involved, and neither have social workers – they could not provide a full service for these patients. So, unless, or until, another agency is recruited, the police will have to continue as before.

Over the years, the police have tried to meet some of these criticisms, with some forces introducing training programmes for all grades of officers. The Mental Health Act Commission, in their Sixth Biennial Report (1993–95), spoke of improved levels of practice, with new jointly agreed policies, producing improved police awareness and training – occasionally producing an improved level of recording of the use of Section 136, this following the Ritchie Report on Christopher Clunis. One of the best is in the Metropolitan Police, where all operational officers up to the rank of inspector are now given training to help recognise and deal with the mentally disordered. Furthermore, on each division a Mental Health Liaison Officer (MHLO) of supervisory rank liaises with hospitals and other relevant agencies. There is now a useful guide for police officers to help them in their dealings with the mentally disordered (Mental Health Act Commission 1995, para. 8.2). The Commission understands that similar initiatives have been taken elsewhere, although the development is uneven.

The influential Reed Report recommended that police training should cover *all* aspects of the Mental Health Act 1983, including the initial identification of suspects who appear to be mentally disordered. This, it recommended, should be followed by opportunities for refresher training and joint training with other groups working with mentally disordered offenders (Department of Health 1992b, para. 11.197). In particular, the Reed Committee wanted training to help the police to distinguish between patients with learning disabilities and those with mental illness (ibid. para. 11.117). Whether this level of training is necessary is doubtful, given the existing pressure on resources, but Reed clearly saw it as a means by which the police could increase their diagnostic skills.

A key feature of these police programmes, especially that of the Metropolitan Police, is the MHLO. The MHLO, available 24 hours per day, must liaise with other agencies and advise the rank and file constables about how best to deal with the mentally disordered. Inexperienced police officers, unaware of the facilities available, will find contact with a specialist officer rewarding and time saving, increasing the chances of bringing an incident to a successful conclusion. This mentor model, originally developed in the United States, is, I suggest, likely to be more beneficial than the awareness training programmes of the type advanced by Reed, as it offers an approach more in tune with police thinking and practice.

Be that as it may, what is interesting and, it has to be admitted, rather odd about police involvement under Section 136 is that the community safety lobby seem not to have realised the potential for increasing the level and extent of controls. There have been criticisms about the failure of the police to cooperate with other services, a point often brought out in public enquiries. On the other hand, there has been little or no pressure on the police to increase Section 136 detentions, or for more vigilance in their approach. Where criticisms exist, they have, if anything, been the other way round, that is, for the police to be less vigilant and be less assiduous in their duties. There may be many reasons for this: those critics of the police powers may differ from those who demand more community safety; or there may be a lack of enthusiasm for more police involvement generally, so that where an increase in community safety is required, it would be expected to occur through the more traditional psychiatric services. Whatever the reasons, it seems that the police will remain key figures in modern mental health services and with increasing levels of training show that they can meet some of their critics.

The use of the police station as a place of safety

The influential Home Office Circular 66/90 (Home Office 1990) repeated and restated government policy on the use of Section 136: 'It is desirable that, whenever possible, the place of safety in which the person might be detained should be a hospital and not a police station' (para. 4.1). Department of Health guidance on the use of Section 136 says a police station should only be used where a more appropriate place for assessment is not immediately available, or where the person concerned is in transit (Department of Health 1983).

The debate about the use of a police station as a place of safety is long-standing. Clearly, police stations are not places where someone in a distressed condition should be kept for any length of time. The 72 hours permitted in the Act is far too long and, although the Richardson Committee (Richardson 1999, para. 5.42) wanted the time reduced to 24 hours, in my view, six hours should be the maximum. Nor is it appropriate to detain a mentally disordered person alongside an offender, and the fact that many such non-offender patients on a Section 136 have previous convictions is not of itself sufficient justification for detaining them alongside those who have, or for keeping them in conditions similar to those being charged.

On the other hand, Brenda Hoggett (1984) says there is much to be said for taking the patient to the police station so that a properly considered choice may be made between treating him as a medical problem, or as a penal problem, or as no problem at all (p. 139). She thinks that a patient may prefer to have matters sorted out in a police station and then go to a hospital or other place of safety. One obvious advantage of the police station is that it provides physical security in an environment staffed 24 hours per day with constant surveillance. Set this against a local authority facility, often staffed by local authority workers without the necessary support system, and the advantage of the police station becomes clear. Brenda Hoggett believes that most patients prefer a police station to a hospital – the label 'patient' is not thus summarily applied to someone who is later found not to be mentally disordered. There are also legal advantages: patients on a Section 136 order have been arrested which provides them with all the rights under the PACE Act 1984, such as the right to have an Appropriate Adult (see Chapter 6), there being no such right if a hospital is the place of safety. However, this right under PACE is almost never exercised or publicly recognised by custody officers.

There remains, however, the unpalatable fact that arrest and detention in a police station *does* criminalise a mental disorder, which in all other respects is a non-criminal medical condition. Moreover, there are operational examples, too numerous to ignore, where the police use Section 136 as a way of avoiding the more complex procedures under the criminal law. Improvements in training which will lead to better practice is perhaps the best way forward, but even so there will always remain a measure of criminalisation as long as the police are involved.

It is interesting and reassuring that the Richardson Committee, when reviewing the Mental Health Act (Richardson 1999, para. 5.41), said that they heard strong arguments for removing the police station as a place of safety but thought there may be no realistic alternative in remote areas. They recommended that local protocols be developed so that the use of a police station is restricted to cases where there is a serious risk of violence (para. 5.41). At long last a government body has recognised the value in retaining the police station as a place of safety, and has come to terms with an awkward and difficult problem.

In the *Review of the Mental Health Act 1959* (Department of Health/ Home Office 1978), it was stated that, while a hospital will be recommended as the usual 'place of safety', the government was aware of what it called operational difficulties that the police encountered. Often these present as logistical problems but are no less important for that. Finding a hospital prepared to take a patient on a place of safety can be difficult, and if the patient was first detained in a police station, it is unclear if he can be sent to a second place of safety before being seen by the ASW and psychiatrist. In London, mental hospitals are usually some distance from the scene of the disturbance; this involves negotiations with the hospital concerned, and an extensive police involvement. In research conducted in 1983, it was found that the police were dealt with rudely by hospital staff, often being kept waiting for two or three hours, and, on one occasion, when the patient was not accepted by the hospital, he was back in the centre of London before the police came (Rogers 1993). Some of the uglier features of the British class system were on display, where the police were dealt with unfavourably by medical and allied professionals who saw the police, not as colleagues, but as part of a plot to offload the offender/patient onto the hospital.

Some policy implications

In the Review of the 1959 Act (op. cit. 1978), it was said there is an understandable reluctance in some hospitals to act as a place of safety, since staff feel that they are being asked to accept responsibility for the custody and care of someone who is possibly violent or a nuisance, but whose need for treatment has not been assessed. Again, in the research by Anne Rogers (1993) she found some patients were interviewed by medical staff while still in handcuffs. She goes on to say:

There is clearly a widespread impression that the act of removing someone to hospital under Section 136 is tantamount to their formal admission as a patient. In fact the section only authorises a person's removal to a place of safety for the purpose of medical examination and interview by a Mental Welfare Officer (now an Approved Social Worker) and the making of any necessary arrangements for his treatment and care. Once these have taken place the power lapses. (para. 2.26)

The above quote provides a good description of the requirements of Section 136, setting out the procedures to be undertaken. Astonishingly, for most hospitals these still remain unclear, with many of their Codes of Practice hopelessly muddled and confused; many seem to believe that Section 136 is an admission order, which it is not, but a place of safety order. That is, it is an order detaining a patient until a decision has been made about any subsequent treatment and care. Some hospitals, it seems, do not call a social worker, or have the patient assessed by a psychiatrist, as they are required to do.

Why do such difficulties remain? In the Review of the 1959 Act (op. cit. 1978), the point was made that operational difficulties have arisen (and it seems still arise) which cannot be overcome by legislative changes. A Code of Practice was suggested, but has not been introduced; the Home Office Circular 66/90 (Home Office 1990) spoke of the importance of 'establishing close working relationships with local health, probation and social services to assist the police in exercising those powers', but rarely have they been established. Our experience is that more than this is required; 'close working relationships' may take place at the highest administrative levels, but are absent at the grass roots where it matters.

The police themselves are not without criticism. In her research on the use of the Appropriate Adult, Teresa Nemitz (1997) studied over 20,000 police records in selected police stations in the East Midlands. She noticed that numerous custody records recorded the suspect as 'detained under the Mental Health Act' or simply as being 'Mental Health', whatever that might mean. Rarely did the detaining officers or custody officer know or understand what this meant, nor were they familiar with the procedures required under Section 136. More often than not the arresting officer or custody officer referred the suspect to the police surgeon, but as will be shown below, this invariably led to a cursory interview and an assessment of 'fit to be detained, fit to be interviewed'. Exceptionally, a psychiatrist or social worker would be called, but even then there was rarely anything on the custody record to suggest that Section 136 was being invoked, although of course it clearly was. The police stations used in this research may have been an unrepresentative sample, but three police authorities were covered by the study, which included police stations in rural and urban areas, and the response was similar throughout. The police officers were familiar with PACE, but not, it seems, with that part of it concerned with mental disorder, for the Mental Health Act seemed not to be within their compass. If 'close working relationships with other agencies' is to mean anything, it must involve the custody officer, who in practice runs the police station.

One solution is to produce a more effective monitoring system requiring the police to record the use of Section 136, and especially when the police station was used as a 'place of safety'. If nothing else this would make the police aware that this section exists, and help to provide information on the extent of its use. The Metropolitan Police seem to be one of the few police forces that record their admissions, although whether they do so assiduously is not known. (The police areas in which Teresa Nemitz (1997) conducted her research did not record Section 136 for those years under review (1992–93), and one nearby police authority had only one recorded Section 136 since 1960, and that was said to be an error.) The Richardson Committee (1999) also recommended that the police are required to record applications for a Section 136 and send records annually to the Mental Health Act Commission (para. 5.40). Were these monitoring arrangements to be introduced, they could operate alongside the compulsory admission procedures suggested in Chapter 3, and would provide an extensive data set available for analysis by the Mental Health Act Commission and not the Department of Health.

It remains puzzling why after so long there should be misunderstandings about the use of Section 136, why so many hospitals still get it wrong and why the police themselves know so little about it, and this is in spite of numerous government initiatives recommending that the police station not be used as a place of safety, and that a hospital is preferred. That Section 136 is regarded as a hospital admission order compounds the confusion, whether by hospital staff or the police themselves. The custody officer is the key figure here, without his cooperation and goodwill little will change.

Introducing formal procedures would be a way forward, as not only would this direct police officers' attention to the legal requirements of Section 136, it would also show how often it is used. We cannot assume it is not being used in those police areas which record no formal admissions; it is safe to believe that it is used extensively throughout England and Wales, even if unrecorded, and without consideration of the law's demands. Phrases such as 'mental health' were written on so many custody forms in the study as to confirm this, but the procedures that followed had little to do with the legislation itself. That cannot and should not continue, for if nothing else the patients are not given the protection of the law, nor do they receive the appropriate psychiatric examination that the law requires.

A comment is required about the type of person detained under Section 136. The research evidence is incomplete, but in a study carried out in London (Rassaby and Rogers 1987), those detained were at the top end of a psychiatric/offender severity scale, whether in terms of mental condition, or the extent of previous convictions. All were detained in hospital after the Section 136 order expired (except one who was not admitted, he had been in that hospital before and was barred from readmission) and for a longer period than other patients under Sections 2 and 3. Clearly the police were able to identify mental disorder – if anything they concentrated on the severe chronic group rather than 'the worried well', or those with neurotic conditions. In other words, they were key figures in the promotion of community safety.

A comment is also required about the ethnicity of those detained. In the same study (ibid. 1987), most of the patients were white but the black group was significantly overrepresented. It is easy to slip into a simple argument that racial prejudice on behalf of the Metropolitan Police accounted for the overrepresentation. To do so ignores the complexities of the referral process, when more often than not the police were called by the suspect's family – sometimes they had turned him out and he was creating a disturbance or molesting them outside their home. It also ignores the suspect's psychiatric condition, past and present, and the way in which the police were involved in lengthy negotiations with the hospital – mainly with non-white psychiatrists – to get the patient admitted on a place of safety order. It would have been simpler, less time consuming and, as it happens, a good deal more heartless to have charged the suspect under a public order offence, detained him overnight and brought him before a court the next day. The questions to be asked about the overrepresentation of black patients are more complex and include how and why patients, black and otherwise, are brought to the attention of the police, and why some are detained under Section 136 and others not. We have little or no research data on this, but sadly no shortage of anecdotes, assertions and conjecture on what is a very troubling problem. Slogans are no help, nor are politically motivated comments from whichever direction they appear: hard data are worth much more, produced by way of a sophisticated research design.

Again, and at the risk of being overrepetitive, it is difficult to understand why so little research has been done on Section 136, or on Section 135. These sections involve a system of controls involving the detention of a suspect for up to 72 hours. They are of a fundamental nature, that is, and to repeat this point also, the patient can be taken to a place of safety, detained, with no right of appeal, whether against the detention itself or the subsequent decision of the psychiatrist and social worker. Inquiries suggest that medical services in hospitals, and the police, often misunderstand what was required of them. That is bad enough, but worse when one considers that a new Mental Health Act is being proposed, 18 years after the last one, and there is still confusion about a key section such as this.

The Expert Committee (Department of Health 1999) recommended some minor changes, but did not suggest that Section 136 be removed from mental health legislation. It said 'the powers should be retained' but did not want to accept suggestions that the police powers should be extended 'beyond a public place' (para. 5.39). Section 136 is, after all, nothing more than a means whereby the mentally disordered in a public place can be assessed. It offers an alternative means by which the civil powers of Sections 2, 3, and 4 can be exercised.

The Forensic Medical Examiner

In *Core Issues in Policing* (1996), Kathleen Kelly et al. begin by saying that the role and work of the Forensic Medical Examiner (FME) (or police surgeon as they used to be called) does not at first sight conjure up images of a 'core issue in contemporary policing' (p. 160). The authors go on to restate a familiar refrain, that virtually no research had been undertaken on the activities of the FME, which they regard as untenable. They say that the FME does much to bring into play many of the current core issues in policing, to which can be added 'and many in relation to mental disorder also'.

Briefly, the FME is required to provide a forensic and service function. The former need not concern us here; it is about obtaining medical evidence to be used in the trial, involving a variety of activities, including examining suspects when police maltreatment is alleged, or where assaults have occurred. The service function is of greater relevance; for these purposes it is about dealing with the medical and psychiatric needs of the suspect. That the two functions often overlap is obvious; forensic questions can be service orientated, and service functions have a forensic input. Here, however, we shall concentrate on the service functions, especially those concerned with the diagnosis and disposal of the mentally disordered.

There are between 1,500–2,000 FMEs in Britain, of whom only about 9% are full time and almost all are GPs. No one really knows the exact number, as research by the Home Office shows that about 900 of those are appointed on a part-time contractual basis and data on these are not collected (Audit Commission 1998, p. 8). As part of the Reed Committee's overview concerning the development of psychiatric services, the Committee wanted FMEs to provide a comprehensive system of psychiatric care. The Committee (Department of Health 1992b) recommended that:

> There should be closer links between FMEs and local psychiatric services to ensure that the needs of mentally disordered people detained in police custody are addressed with urgency and that FMEs are encouraged to develop a better understanding of the needs of mentally disordered offenders. We suggest that the establishment of specialist panels may assist FMEs to acquire relevant experience. (para 11.4)

In fact, FMEs are rather solitary figures, they have no central coordinating group, although they have their own professional association. The local police authority employs each FME. As most of the FMEs are part-time GPs, there is also the problem of producing consistency, or interrater reliability in their assessments, and of achieving high levels of psychiatric competency in an increasingly sophisticated medical world.

There is little doubt that FMEs are key figures. The Codes of Practice under PACE define the FME's role; Section 66 of PACE requires the custody officer to call an FME if a person brought to a police station or already detained there appears to be suffering from a mental (or physical) disorder. In urgent cases, the suspect must be sent to a hospital. These apply even if the suspect makes no request for medical attention (Home Office 1990, para. 4(iv)). Clearly, their potential to influence events is large, but before examining that, we will consider what FMEs do and how they do it.

They see a variety of suspects, but the numbers and types of patient are unknown, for no central record is kept. The Audit Commission says that the increasing reliance upon community-based care for mentally ill people, and the growth of a drug culture, are having an impact on the work of the FME (1998, para. 6). A study carried out in 1992 suggested that FMEs working in the Metropolitan district were called out to see 1 prisoner in 4, the average for provincial stations was 1 in 9, with 1 in 10 for Suffolk and 1 in 20 for Devon and Cornwall (quoted in ibid. para. 14). The custody officer is the key; the discretion exercised by custody officers accounting for the variations, where less experienced custody officers used their discretion the least.

Interviews, it seems, are short, with the outcome fairly predictable. Evidence to the Royal Commission on Criminal Justice (1992) showed that 60% of all police surgeons had taken 10 minutes or less to complete their medical examination and in only 6% of the cases did they take more than one hour. The length of time taken does not determine the quality of the interview, except that there are expectations on FMEs which suggest that they should be involved in something much more extensive. The Royal Commission, concerned as it was about the quality of service to offenders, said that:

> if a comprehensive mental and physical state examination were to become a necessary part of fitness for interview and assessment many police surgeons would need to spend much more time than they do at present in the police station. (p. 18)

The Royal Commission thought that the FME's decision was based more on intuitive clinical variables than on sound identification and examination of clinical facts (p. 12). This stinging criticism has had considerable impact – at least on the FME's professional association, if not always on its members.

In a review of existing FME practices and using a small number of case histories taken from an inner city police station in Derby, two features of the FME's work were examined. (The study was with drug offenders but the results are relevant for mental health.) First, the length of time taken for the interview, and second, the way FMEs determine outcome, in this case deciding whether a patient is 'fit to be detained and fit to be interviewed'. The research confirmed the data given to the Royal Commission (Bean and Nemitz 1997). The average length of time for interview was just over five minutes, with the content often perfunctary. Moreover, the then Notification of Addict Regulations required 'any doctor who attends a person who he considers or has reasonable grounds to suspect is addicted to a controlled drug to notify the Home Office Addicts Index'. Twenty-five recorded case histories of drug users, known to and treated by the FMEs and checked with the Addicts Index, were examined. None were notified (see Home Office 1994, para. 9.13).

How FMEs determine outcome was equally interesting. Evidence to the Royal Commission (1992) found that only 3% of drug users seen were said to be unfit to be detained. Bean and Nemitz produced similar results and suggested that 'fit to be detained, fit to be interviewed' was a standard, speedy response for almost all interviews, and for almost all circumstances, including mental disorder. The PACE Code of Practice says an offender will not be fit if he is

> unfit through drink or drugs to the extent that he is unable to appreciate the significance of questions put to him and his answers may be questioned about an alleged offence in that condition. (quoted in Home Office 1994, para 9.4)

Everyone who was seen by the FME was found 'fit to be detained, fit to be interviewed' – an almost standard response (Bean and Nemitz 1997).

Margaret Stark, who often speaks for the FME Association, argues that an FME has to be able to answer the following questions about fitness for interview – this again in terms of substance abuse.

1 Is there evidence of drug abuse?
2 Is the patient currently under the influence of drugs or alcohol?
3 Is the patient fully aware of his surroundings with unimpaired judgements and in a fit condition to cope with a stressful interview, understand questions put to him and to instruct solicitors?

These questions, she says, are now being answered adequately by FMEs in their examination of offenders and, while standards may not always have been high in the past, there is evidence of real change (Stark 1994).

It may, however, be too late. Criticism of FMEs are increasing, and questions are being asked about whether they give value for money (for details of fees charged see Bean and Nemitz 1997 and the Audit Commission 1998, paras 7–9). In some parts of London, the Metropolitan Police are assigning many of the tasks once reserved for FMEs to nurses, especially for those patients having minor cuts and abrasions. Nurses seem to be give more value for money.

Returning to questions of mental disorder; PACE requires the FME to be called whenever a suspect appears to be mentally disordered (Code 9.2). The FME must then make various decisions *inter alia* to decide whether suspects remain in the criminal justice system, or are diverted to the psychiatric services, or whether psychiatric treatment is required at that stage. As with the Appropriate Adult, there is no reason why the activities of the FME should not be included in mental health legislation; the FME's decisions have a long-term ripple effect throughout the criminal justice system and beyond. It is the FME who advises the police on the direction in which they should proceed for mentally disordered patients. Existing legislation is not directive enough; FMEs are given wide discretionary powers, whether in terms of the interview, the decisions they make and the suspects they see. That so few have any specialist qualifications in the treatment and diagnosis of mental disorder is itself a further failing.

The procedures followed, at least in the police stations observed as part of the Appropriate Adult research (Bean and Nemitz 1994), were along the following lines; first, a suspect thought to be mentally disordered was referred to the FME (some suspects were listed on the police records as receiving psychiatric treatment, some as 'schizophrenic', others as 'subnormal' or 'mentally handicapped'. Presumably the police obtained this information from relatives or suspects or witnesses). The suspect was briefly interviewed and invariably determined 'fit to be detained, fit to be interviewed'. Only very rarely – perhaps fewer than 1% of the cases – was the suspect referred to a psychiatrist, in spite of the police records noting the existence of a current psychiatric condition or similar.

If the procedures observed are representative of the FME's actions generally, then we have the genesis of the large number of mentally disordered offenders in the criminal justice system. The opportunity to note, mark, record, refer for treatment and begin treatment for that disorder is in the police stations, but it is missed. As a result, many mentally disordered offenders enter the system unnoticed, untreated and with no record of their disorder.

'Fit to be detained, fit to be interviewed' is not an assessment of mental disorder, it is an assessment of mental capacity. Suspects may be 'fit to be detained, fit to be interviewed' and be mentally disordered, but they may not. If a person is 'unfit to be detained, unfit to be interviewed' it is probable that he is mentally disordered – it is rare to be otherwise – but mental disorder and mental incapacity are not synonymous (Grisso and Applebaum 1988). FMEs appear not to notice this, or if they do, they are content to assess mental capacity in spite of the Codes of Practice suggesting otherwise.

From the police perspective, this may not matter. There remains a functional dependency between the police and FMEs which is difficult to break. FMEs are monopoly providers in a market which pays very well for their services. They are punctilious attendees. They grant the police a professional medical opinion which protects them and allows them to continue with their interviews. Put differently, they get the police off the hook. When FMEs pronounce an offender 'fit to be detained, fit to be interviewed', they permit the police to proceed, unhindered by external medical considerations. That this opinion is worth less than the police believe (see also Chapter 6 on Appropriate Adults for an example) is neither here nor there. They can always say that professional opinions were sought on matters outside their knowledge and, once given, they proceeded accordingly.

FMEs grant the police a measure of professional competency which allows the police to process a suspect through the police station, unhindered by other medical or psychiatric questions. If the FME says 'fit to be detained, fit to be interviewed', then so be it. Only very occasionally are the FME's views ignored or bypassed. In one police station in a relatively small town in Lincolnshire, the custody officer referred some suspects directly to the psychiatrist, with others diverted out of the criminal justice system to various treatment agencies. Why was the FME not called? The custody officer said he knew these suspects, knew their families, and had processed them many times before. A professional (medical) opinion was not necessary, that is to say, the custody officer was confident in his own judgement about the offender (Nemitz 1997).

The role of the FME cries out for more research. Questions as to how and under what circumstances FMEs are called, how they make their decisions and what the effects of these decisions are on the subsequent careers of the mentally disordered offender need to be answered. As shown later in Chapter 8 on dual diagnosis, FMEs should pick up these cases as they go through the system and alert the treatment services in the criminal justice system. Above all, FMEs should be given more direction. Kelly et al. (1996) talk of professional dominance, that is, most FMEs believe that their qualification as GPs is sufficient experience for the role of FME. Paradoxically, a qualification in general practice means that the FME is vastly overqualified for much of what he does, yet vastly underqualified in other areas: overqualified in that much of the work involves medical trivia which could be undertaken by a qualified nurse, and underqualified when he is required to make sophisticated diagnoses involving mental disorder, substance abuse or a combination of the two. Hence, the likelihood and increasing possibility of providing a less than adequate service.

The Audit Commission (1998), in a comprehensive review of FME practices, made detailed recommendations about recruitment, training and the management of forensic medical services, which, if implemented, would greatly assist and reduce some of the more pressing problems. At a cost of over £20 million per year, these services are expensive, but how much more expensive are the decisions made by

FMEs for the criminal justice system? What began in 1830, with the appointment of a doctor to examine potential recruits to the newly established Metropolitan Police force, and led to the development of the NHS involving the police surgeon as physician to police officers and their families has now grown to involve duties imposed by PACE. Their role and function is hardly recognisable (ibid. p. 6). The time has come to take a closer look and examine the implications of what FMEs do, whether in the police station or beyond.

Conclusion

In the first part of this chapter, an examination was made of the way Section 136 operates. The police powers under Section 136 have been heavily criticised, not so much for what they are but for the fact that the police themselves are required to detain the mentally disordered in a public place, and take them to a police station which can act as a place of safety. There may be many regrets about police involvement, and those regrets are likely to be shared by the police themselves, but no other occupational group could offer such a service. Like it or not, the police will remain key figures in the primary care services. The decarceration movement and the drift to community care increases police involvement, so the question is not so much about whether the police should be involved, but how much. They, alongside social services, have been criticised by a number of public inquiries mainly for failing to cooperate with other services, and the community safety lobby has not been slow to point out these failings. Improved cooperation at all levels may help, as will improved training along the lines offered by the Metropolitan Police.

The second part of the chapter concentrated on the FME, who occupies a key position in the police station and makes important decisions about the numerous patients he is called upon to examine. Whether a patient finishes up in the criminal justice system or the mental health system is often determined by the actions of the FME. Given the often perfunctory nature of the interview, that decision is by default, rather than by design.

It is here that the integrity of the mental health system needs to be reasserted. Few patients, it seems, receive a careful assessment of their condition, and many are left to enter the criminal justice system without a clear assessment of their condition, other than being told they were 'fit for interview'. It is not clear how this situation can be remedied; is it the responsibility of the police to change things, or of government, or of the FMEs themselves? The answer is, probably all three, in which case the arrangements to change the 1983 Act need to include an examination of the future role of FMEs as they affect the mentally disordered in the police station, a matter which is also the subject of the next chapter.

6

Appropriate Adults and Mentally Disordered Suspects in Police Stations

This chapter is central to what I have called maintaining the integrity of mental health, and follows on from the second part of Chapter 5. It is about preserving, or rather sustaining and developing, the rights of mentally disordered suspects (or offenders, the terms have been used interchangeably) in police stations. In an age where community safety dominates, there is a tendency to trample over these rights of the unloved and the unlovely according to Herschel Prins, and to forget that their rights are worth preserving. In this chapter, an examination will be made of one way in which those rights are promoted, that is, through the so-called Appropriate Adult. The Appropriate Adult is there to protect the mentally disordered while being questioned by the police, and to help to prevent miscarriages of justice.

Current mental health legislation does not include specific provisions for the protection of the mentally disordered in police stations. This is provided elsewhere, formerly in the Judges Rules, now under the Police and Criminal Evidence Act 1984 (PACE). There has always been a need to protect this vulnerable group, whether from unfair questioning or from being intimidated, or from producing confessions which may turn out to be false. Indeed, the Codes of Practice concerned with the mentally disordered in police custody draw attention to the special care that should always be exercised when questioning a mentally disordered person. These offenders are prone to provide information which is unreliable, misleading, or self-incriminating (Codes of Practice C, Annex E3). There is no reason why the current provisions should not be refined, updated and included in any new legislation, for somewhere between 10% and 15% of all suspects in police stations are mentally disordered, whether severe or otherwise. Protection is required for this vulnerable group, and protection in this context means securing the rights of suspects while being interviewed.

Existing legal provisions are found in the Guidelines to PACE, which set out the manner in which the police and others are to deal with mentally disordered suspects in the police station. They involve the use of the so-called Appropriate Adult, whose task is to protect the mentally disordered (and others defined as vulnerable, such as the partially sighted, the deaf, those not able to speak and those unable to understand English). Were these provisions to work as intended, they would have a significant impact on the way the mentally disordered are dealt with in the criminal justice system; as it is, Appropriate Adults are rarely used, in spite of the extensive requirements in PACE, leaving many mentally disordered without protection or without their rights secured.

Background to the Appropriate Adult in PACE

There is little doubt that suspects brought to the police station for questioning are in a vulnerable position; the police station is not a neutral place, it offers an environment favourable to the police, who are on their home territory. The police determine the speed, content and direction of proceedings, and know most, if not all, of the rules. All suspects faced with the prospect of being interviewed in a police station must find it daunting: how much more so for the mentally disordered, and others who are vulnerable (McConville et al. 1991).

Not surprisingly then, over the years some spectacular cases of injustice have arisen. One of the most famous concerned that of Maxwell Confait, a homosexual transvestite found murdered in a house in Lewisham, south London, in April 1972. He had been strangled. Three youths were convicted of the murder; one of them, aged 18, had a mental age of 8 years and was described by a psychiatrist as 'very markedly suggestible so that the slightest indication of the expected answer will produce it' (Price and Caplan 1977). Another, aged 15, was assessed as emotionally disturbed and of borderline intelligence. The third, although of reasonable intelligence, had only just turned 14, was Turkish and had difficulty with English. Three years later, the Home Secretary was persuaded to reopen their case and the Court of Appeal declared them innocent (ibid. 1977). In another case in Newcastle upon Tyne, Paul Hails, a 23-year-old labourer, was found guilty of sexual assault, he was mentally subnormal, and convicted mainly on the evidence of his confession. He was sent to Rampton Special

Hospital. Later, two others admitted to the murder and the Court of Appeal quashed his conviction. These and other similar cases prompted *The Times* to talk of 'disquieting miscarriages of justice' (6 August 1992), which may not be commonplace but are sufficiently frequent to raise questions about the way mentally disordered persons in police stations are dealt with when convicted on uncorroborated confessions. The Confait case also illustrated that, once the confession had been made, other evidence was seen as less important. Once convicted, the difficulties in securing a successful appeal become immense – there are mountains to climb to get a Home Secretary to reopen a case.

In the Confait case, it was held that the police, in their eagerness to obtain confessions, were overzealous, and the confessions, on which they placed great store, false. Confait was about more than this: other aspects of the proceedings were defective. The forensic medical evidence was poorly obtained and the summing up by the trial judge less than unbiased. The first Court of Appeal followed this by saying that no misdirection had occurred. The Confait case put British justice under scrutiny, not for the first time, for, as Brenda Hoggett (1984) observes, English law cuts a poor figure when dealing with the mentally disordered, and never more so than in the Confait case.

Some of the solutions produced by the Confait case are found in PACE, that is to say, the Appropriate Adult is now given a firmer base on which to proceed. Even so, the rules are often ambiguous, while the courts seem not too concerned about whether an Appropriate Adult was used and rarely dismiss cases when an Appropriate Adult was not, although this may be slowly changing. The police and the FMEs seem ill prepared, often not knowing the law and often appearing to confuse the Appropriate Adult with provisions under Section 136. How should mentally disordered suspects be interviewed, and how should they fit into the criminal justice system – a system incidentally which starts with the assumption that all suspects are competent to make rational assessments unless proven otherwise? How are those who are not competent to cope with proceedings to be dealt with when being questioned in the police station?

The Appropriate Adult provisions

The influential Home Office Circular 66/90 (Home Office 1990) sets out the aims and provisions for dealing with mentally disordered offenders in police stations generally:

the questioning of (Mentally Disordered Offenders) suspected of committing offences as subject to the Code of Practice for the Detention, Treatment and Questioning of Persons by Police Officers issued under Section 66 of the PACE 1984, Paragraph 9.2 (of the Code), requires the custody officer immediately to call a police surgeon if a person brought to a police station or already detained there appears to be suffering from mental disorder. (para. 4(iv))

The Circular is, however, strangely silent on the use of the Appropriate Adult, which is odd because PACE has been in operation since 1984, six years before the Circular. When the Home Office fails to give prominence to the Appropriate Adult, it is hardly likely that the police will do otherwise, and equally likely that they will fail to understand its provisions.

PACE and the Codes of Practice succeeded the earlier Judges Rules, which were in place at the time of the Confait case. Code C, which now includes the Revised Codes of Practice under PACE, sets out the Rules and Guidelines, including the detention and interviewing of mentally abnormal suspects. The most important is:

> If an officer has any suspicion, or is told in good faith that a person of any age may be mentally incapable of understanding the significance of questions put to him or his replies, then that person shall be treated as a mentally disordered or mentally handicapped person for the purposes of the Code. (Code 1.4 Codes of Practice)

Being defined as mentally disordered means *inter alia* that an Appropriate Adult must be informed of the suspect's detention and asked to attend a police station. The Code says an Appropriate Adult may be a relative or Guardian, or someone experienced in dealing with the mentally disordered or handicapped persons. The Revised Code advises that an ASW as defined under the 1993 Act or a specialist social worker, or some other responsible adult could act as an Appropriate Adult (Code 1.7). Other than in exceptionally urgent circumstances, interviews with mentally disordered suspects must take place in the presence of an Appropriate Adult (Code 11.4). Appropriate Adults must be informed that their role during police interviews is not to act simply as an observer but to assist the suspect and determine that questioning is conducted fairly, and facilitate communication (Code 11.6). Finally, Appropriate Adults must ensure that the rights of the suspect are respected and that the testimony given to the police is reliable.

Extensive duties are given to an Appropriate Adult, and to repeat the point: there is no other protection for the mentally disordered at this stage of the proceedings, except of course when the suspect is legally represented. Without commenting too closely on the quality of legal representation, it would appear that, according to John Baldwin (1982), it is occasionally uncertain and often variable.

The first question is an empirical one: do police use the Appropriate Adult? The answer is, very rarely. In a study of five police stations involving detailed examination of 20,805 custody records, the Appropriate Adult was used only 38 times (Bean and Nemitz 1993; Nemitz 1997). On the basis of the expected rate of mental disorder, that is, about 11% of all suspects in a police station, there should have been about 2,300 suspects where an Appropriate Adult should have been called; at the lower expected rate of 7%, there should have been about 1,350.

The three case histories given below are taken from records in police stations in the East Midlands (Nemitz 1997). They show the levels of uncertainty and misunderstanding by the police when dealing with mentally disordered suspects. They also show in broad outline how the system works and help to identify some of its key features.

In Case A, the FME was telephoned by the custody sergeant to gain information about medication in the suspect's property, which was eventually identified as Largactil and Heminevrin tablets. The FME informed the custody sergeant that 'these tablets are only prescribed to persons who are suffering from severe mental problems'. This information alerted the custody officer who then contacted the Emergency Duty Team to send a social worker to act as an Appropriate Adult. But due to the lateness of the hour (00.55 a.m.), it was agreed to conduct the PACE interview the following day. An ASW finally attended the police station at 15.00 p.m. the next day, and an interview was conducted in the presence of a solicitor which lasted for 30 minutes. The suspect was arrested on suspicion of rape, but was released from custody because of insufficient evidence. The FME did not examine the suspect; he attended only to authorise the administration of the medication. This suspect was detained in custody for approximately 18 hours.

In Case B, this suspect's probation officer informed the custody sergeant that her client had 'learning difficulties' and that she must be present to act as the Appropriate Adult when interviewed, as indeed she was. A few days later this suspect was subsequently 'breached' by the same probation officer and was arrested in the probation officer's office. Yet for the 'breach' it was not thought necessary for the suspect to have the special protection of an Appropriate Adult. This case highlights conflicts of interest that may arise when a professional involved with the suspect/client takes on the dual role of care worker and controller. It also shows how the role of the Appropriate Adult should be wider than currently defined. Are not interviews by the probation officer of similar standing to those of the police? One would think so, as are all interviews with the mentally disordered, which could lead to a loss of freedom.

In Case C, this suspect told his solicitor that he had twice attempted suicide using sleeping pills; he had amitriptyline tablets in his possession. The custody sergeant telephoned the FME who said this medication was 'not controlled and two tablets may be given safely'. The tablets were given at 12.00 noon; the suspect had been in custody since 10.30 a.m. The next day the solicitor arrived at 10.22 a.m. and an ASW arrived at 12.47 p.m. There was no information on the custody record about who called the social worker except this statement, which said 'seen by social worker under Mental Health Act'. At 13.14 p.m. a psychiatrist attended the police station 'at the request of social services'. No mental health assessment was recorded; the next day the suspect went to court and was given a conditional discharge for 12 months, and 'handed over to Mr (name of social worker), social worker'.

In C above, it was the solicitor not the custody officer who was sufficiently concerned for his client's welfare and it was he who urged the attendance of a social worker. Was the social worker acting as an Appropriate Adult and/or carrying out a Mental Health Act assessment? It was difficult to say. Was the psychiatrist acting as an Appropriate Adult? Again, it was difficult to say. Notice in the case above that the use of an Appropriate Adult was linked to an assessment under Section 136, as if it was a way of transferring the suspect to psychiatric care. That the Appropriate Adult and Section 136 are linked in law is correct, but not as shown in the above example. PACE says an Appropriate Adult should be used in Section 136 cases whenever a police station is used as a place of safety: the suspect is arrested under this section of the Act. No examples were found where an Appropriate Adult was used in Section 136 cases (Nemitz 1997).

Generally speaking then, it was not so much that an Appropriate Adult was rarely used, but that there seemed to be little or no understanding by the police of the role or function of the Appropriate Adult. Social workers were no more clear about what they had to do, and neither were the FMEs. The wonder is that the courts are not throwing out more cases; were they to do so, it might encourage the police to take the matter more seriously. In the meantime there are obstacles to be overcome, brought about by serious defects in the way the Guidelines are drafted. If an Appropriate Adult scheme is to work successfully, more thought needs to be given to the way Appropriate Adults should operate, and basic questions answered, such as who should have an Appropriate Adult, who should be an Appropriate Adult, and what should an Appropriate Adult do? Before examining these questions, the role of the custody officer is considered, for he is a key figure in the proceedings; it is the custody officer who makes the decision to call the Appropriate Adult.

The role of the custody officer

According to the Guidelines, the custody officer's task is to:

(a) identify suspects as being mentally disordered, and
(b) initiate proceedings to bring in the Appropriate Adult, and
(c) inform the Appropriate Adult of his/her role and function.

In the first and second of the custody officer's tasks, a common complaint is that the police are unable to identify the mentally disordered. As with Section 136 above, the Guidelines do not require custody officers to diagnose mental disorder at a sophisticated level; they are required to do no more than identify the suspects they believe to be mentally disordered. They are not required to distinguish between the various types of mental disorder, that is, mental illness, psychopathy, learning disability (mental handicap) and so on, or to say whether treatment is required. The task is neither onerous nor does it require special training, and the police seem well able to undertake it. Why then do they rarely call the Appropriate Adult?

What seems to be happening is that custody officers invariably assume that Appropriate Adults are for juveniles, in spite of the Codes of Practice which have been available for a number of years. In effect, calling an Appropriate Adult to a police station for most custody officers means calling a parent or perhaps a social worker to act *in loco parentis*. (Incidentally, whether these parents act as an Appropriate Adult in the true legal sense is difficult to say. Parents seem to come in two forms: one is the 'he-didn't-do-it-and-the-police-are-not-to-be-trusted' variety, and the other is the 'wait-till-I-get-you-home' version. The former hardly encourages cooperation with the police – and what this approach does for the child's respect for authority is another matter – and the latter leaves the parents so much on the side of the police that they fail to protect their child's rights.) One of the best examples showing how the

Appropriate Adult is seen to be only for children occurred in Sheffield in 1993. An existing Appropriate Adult scheme was put out to tender by the local social services department and, when it was taken over by Dr Barnardo's, it was promptly closed for adults (Nemitz 1997, p. 44).

It is suspected that custody officers do not call an Appropriate Adult because they also assume, mistakenly, that the decision to do so is a medical one. When they believe a suspect to be mentally disordered, they refer him to the FME who conducts a medical examination and makes a medical recommendation. That has the effect of producing a definitive professional assessment. So, if an offender is mentally disordered, he might be referred to the psychiatric services: conversely, if the FME sees him and declares him 'fit to be detained and fit to be interviewed', as he almost certainly will, he remains in the criminal justice system. The police have done their duty and have covered themselves in the event of a complaint, having sought professional advice. The error is, of course, clear. The decision to call an Appropriate Adult is not a medical one, if it was, there would be no need for an Appropriate Adult in the first place. Even if the offender was 'fit to be detained', an Appropriate Adult should still be called. A suspect with learning difficulties, or a psychotic patient currently in remission, may well be 'fit to be detained' but remains mentally disordered within the meaning of the Code of Practice. The Code says that he still needs an Appropriate Adult to protect his/her rights during an interview. (One may, of course, question the wisdom of this. If a mentally disordered person is pronounced by the FME 'fit to be interviewed', is there any justification for him having additional protection to the rest of us in the same position? That, however, is an interesting question about mental capacity but it is not what the law says.)

It is also suspected that there is pressure on the custody officer's time, so that to call an Appropriate Adult is to place additional demands on custody officers. It adds pressure because it involves making arrangements, Appropriate Adults may not be easy to contact or be tardy about attendance. The average time recorded before an Appropriate Adult attended the police station in the MENCAP research (Bean and Nemitz 1993) was 3 hours, with a range between 1 and 18 hours. Contrast this with the FMEs, who invariably attended within the hour, and, incidentally, convey the impression that they are on the side of the police. In a busy police station, custody officers will look towards those who provide help, in this case the FME, rather than to those who make extra work.

In Teresa Nemitz's research (1997), she was unable to find any examples concerning the third of the custody officer's duties, that is, to inform the

Appropriate Adult about his role during the police interview as required under the Code of Practice 11.16, and to inform the Appropriate Adult whenever the custody officer has authorised the detention of a mentally disordered person. It is also the duty of the custody officer to prevent the suspect signing a written statement without an Appropriate Adult present. If the custody officer charges a mentally disordered person with an offence, this must be done in the presence of the Appropriate Adult: so too must an intimate body search of the subject.

Presumably, if custody officers are unaware of their first duty, which is to identify offenders who are mentally disordered, they will be unaware of their other duties. Or, perhaps being unwilling to have an Appropriate Adult in the custody suite, they believe the less assistance offered the better. Yet PACE has given the custody officer a certain prominence. Without his cooperation, the system fails. It is difficult to see how those defects can be removed; were the courts to dismiss more cases, that would place pressure on the police, but so too would clear Guidelines from the Home Office. Unless and until that happens, we will continue to muddle along in the same uncertain way.

Who should have an Appropriate Adult?

In a legal sense, an Appropriate Adult should be for anyone who is mentally disordered within the meaning of the 1983 Mental Health Act, and anyone under Section 136 who is brought to a police station on a 'place of safety' order. However, the sheer impracticality of these requirements is obvious. If 10% of all offenders in police stations are mentally disordered, then many thousands of Appropriate Adult interviews will be required annually. The Appropriate Adult's task, however, does not end in the police station, it continues up to and includes the trial; the Appropriate Adult can be called to give evidence about any matter discussed with the offender. (This, incidentally, was exemplified in the famous case of Rosemary West in 1995, where an Appropriate Adult had been allocated to her husband, Frederick West, who committed suicide while on remand. The Appropriate Adult was called to give evidence in Rosemary West's trial. Appropriate Adults are not privileged: and they can, it seems, also sell their information to the press.)

As few Appropriate Adults are used, the problem does not arise, but, as and when there is an increase, decisions will have to be made about which suspects are to be included and which not. Two possibilities exist: either to decide on the basis of the offence, or on the mental/vulnerable condition of the suspect – serious offence *or* serious condition – in practical terms, it cannot be both. The preference here would be for the former: that is, serious offence rather than serious condition. Clearly, the consequences are greater if wrongful convictions occurred, but injustices for a minor offence are no less injustices. However, practical considerations should, I think, take precedence.

Part of the muddle we get ourselves into relates to definitions of mental disorder as provided in the Codes. We are not clear about what we mean by it. For example, under the Code, mental disorder is defined as in Section 1(2) of the 1983 Act as 'mental illness, arrested or incomplete development of mind, psychopathic disorder and any other disorder of the mind'. Thus, the Code includes the psychopath who may be highly intelligent, well aware of what is going on and well able to understand the significance of the questions put to him. Of itself that is bad enough, but para. 1.6 of the Code then extends the definition of mental disorder to include 'the vulnerable' that is, 'the deaf, the partially sighted, those unable to understand English' and so on. On that basis, about 25% of all suspects would qualify for an Appropriate Adult, with some well able to look after themselves and others desperate for assistance. We find ourselves in that position because the Royal Commission on Criminal Procedure (1981), which led to PACE, failed to look at the consequences of its recommendations and walked round the problems in its eagerness to find solutions. What it did was dust down from the shelf an existing definition of mental disorder and add to it the 'vulnerable'. Hardly a satisfactory way of going about things.

Who should the Appropriate Adult be?

The second question is who should the Appropriate Adult be, and, following this, to whom should the Appropriate Adult be responsible in the organisational sense, that is, who should own any scheme? Clearly, the police cannot, although in one northern city (Nemitz 1997), in exasperation at being unable to call an Appropriate Adult, the police trained their own volunteers. This was not successful, because the police thought that the Appropriate Adult's task was to look after the offender's welfare, which in this context meant health and general wellbeing, and not desirable, because the scheme lacked independence. The police, who owned the scheme, could place limitations upon it, as indeed they did, when, for example, they made it clear that they did not expect their Appropriate Adults to interrupt interviews (when one did, the police officer excluded him from that and subsequent interviews, and asked for and was given another Appropriate Adult). Nor did the police expect the Appropriate Adults to challenge their line of questioning, or expect the interview to be terminated when the questioning became unacceptable.

There are a number of local schemes run by MENCAP and MIND, which do not provide long-term solutions but they do offer various prototypes before a national scheme can be introduced. The best model for any national scheme would be that of Victim Support, which is nationally and locally administered, and where local volunteers are recruited to service local areas. A national scheme is preferred to local schemes; the variations are less, with national coverage less uneven. A nationally administered scheme could also be responsible for training.

In the research discussed above, a wide variety of people were called upon to act as Appropriate Adults (Nemitz 1997). Some were parents and family, some were probation officers, some social workers, and others volunteers attached to local mental health organisations. Rarely had the volunteers been trained – even if someone had the knowledge to train them. The Codes say the Appropriate Adult can be:

A relative, guardian, or other person responsible for his care or custody, or someone who has experience of dealing with the mentally disordered who is not a police officer or employed by the police, or some other responsible adult aged 18 or over. (para. 1.7(b))

This creates the impression that anyone can turn up and be an Appropriate Adult, when in fact it is a highly skilled task. Clear signals must be given about the type of people who could become Appropriate Adults. At the time of writing, most schemes are staffed by volunteers offering a range of expertise. There is no central recruiting agency nor are there data on the volunteers – research suggests that some could be regarded as acceptable, others not (Bean and Nemitz 1993).

There are important ethical and moral questions here. Should an Appropriate Adult be appointed who has previous criminal convictions, or is currently receiving psychiatric treatment? Are such people acceptable as Appropriate Adults? Among other things, are they able to stand up to the demands of the task, that is, the possibilities of attending numerous interviews, attending lengthy court trials and being cross-examined in court? Probably not, but that is not a fashionable answer nowadays in this age of user participation.

We must be clear about whose rights we are protecting. Some agencies may want to take advantage of users because they want to use their life experiences, or they do not want to appear to discriminate, and of course, it all depends on the extent and nature of those convictions or of the current psychiatric condition. However, we need to be reminded that the rights we are protecting are of the suspect in the police station, and not of the applicant wanting to be an Appropriate Adult. What happens if the volunteer is not acceptable to the police, who may know him or her under different circumstances? The police will not cooperate, and may not allow him into the police station. What too, if the volunteer is unable to stand up to vigorous and lengthy cross-examination in the witness box? What happens then to the suspect? Moreover, if the Appropriate Adult scheme is to be accepted, it must send out the right signals to the police, the courts and the public generally. If and when a national Appropriate Adult scheme becomes established, it could perhaps take rather more risks, but in the early stages it should not do so.

Two examples will illustrate the point. The first is from MENCAP, who employed an Appropriate Adult for someone charged, with others, with being in a paedophile ring. The harrowing nature of the material produced as evidence, the lengthy trial and the subsequent cross-examinations are vividly described as an ordeal with long-lasting effects. This Appropriate Adult made it clear that stamina and a strong constitution were the order of the day. The second is from the Rosemary West trial, where an Appropriate Adult had been appointed for Frederick West. This Appropriate Adult failed under cross-examination, when it was revealed that she had been offered large sums of money to 'tell all' to a tabloid newspaper.

A previous conviction or a previous psychiatric condition should not automatically bar an applicant from being an Appropriate Adult, although a serious and recent conviction should do so as a matter of course, as should a current serious psychiatric condition. Each case must be taken on its merits and set against the main aim, which is to protect the rights of the suspect, and if that means some applicants are adjudged less than satisfactory, then so be it.

Yet who is appropriate to be an Appropriate Adult remains a fundamental question. Appropriateness involves being able to assert the rights of suspects and protect them whenever they are violated. It involves knowing the rules, and exercising judgement about when and where to intervene. Family members may be willing, but may not always be competent. They may know that things are not as they should be, but may not know how best to intervene – and if the offence was against another family member, that adds to the complexity of things. Nor would 'some other responsible adult' be likely to do much better: being an Appropriate Adult is no task for the well meaning, it is for the person who is aware of his/her duties and obligations, and prepared to give up the necessary time.

Would a lawyer or social worker be better? In Australia, a lawyer is used, but there are complications, especially when the suspect is legally represented. Lawyers are well suited to the setting and knowledgeable about the task in hand, but not all will be prepared to do it – it is, after all, a voluntary post. Would social workers be any better? The Code thinks so, but might there not be a conflict of interest as the task of the ASW under the Mental Health Act is to help with diagnosis and treatment? Protecting rights is a different matter.

It would seem that the most appropriate Appropriate Adult will be a volunteer, who has been trained, who is part of a local scheme servicing a local police area, which is independent of, yet trusted by, the police and is able to provide a 24-hour service. Unfortunately, these volunteers are few and far between, but without them suspects will lack the protection awarded by PACE, and with every likelihood that another case similar to Confait is just around the corner.

What should the Appropriate Adult do?

The duties of the Appropriate Adult involve 'observing that the questioning is conducted fairly and facilitating communication'. The Code of Practice says 'the Appropriate Adult is not expected to act simply as an observer'. If the Appropriate Adult believes the interview is not being conducted fairly, he may interrupt it. Yet, as John Baldwin (1982) says, there is no legal definition of what constitutes a fair interview or fair questioning. Is raising one's voice unfair, or repeating the question unfair, or refusing to accept a negative answer unfair? Is it unfair if there are more than two police officers present? Are the games the police play fair or not, for example when one acts as a kind and attentive officer while the other is more unpleasant (see McConville et al. 1991, p. 68)? And what of 'facilitating communication'? What does that mean? Does it mean interrupting the interview to explain to the offender what is happening? Probably yes, but many police officers will find that not to their liking. Many officers in the research said the Appropriate Adult should never interrupt interviews, except perhaps for 'welfare' reasons such as giving food or drink or allowing the offender to go to the lavatory (Bean and Nemitz 1993).

To muddy the waters further, what of the suspect's lawyer? Are not lawyers there to protect the suspect's rights? If so, how does an Appropriate Adult behave when the suspect is legally represented? Imagine a situation where the police are conducting the interview, the suspect's lawyer is also present, so too is the Appropriate Adult, uninvited by lawyer and suspect, and present with the grudging acceptance of the police. Assume that the Appropriate Adult believes the suspect's rights are not being protected. What then? Under PACE, the Appropriate Adult has a duty to intervene, but it would require a confident Appropriate Adult to do so. Perhaps too much is being made of this, for the research evidence suggests there may be less conflict than expected but McConville et al. (1991) say there is no guarantee that lawyers will protect their client's rights:

> If solicitors are present during interrogations it does not follow that they will 'obstruct' the police. Some will advise their client to speak, even when the answer given constitutes a full admission to the offence under investigation. And some, whilst expressing the intention to protect the client through the use of the right to silence are ineffective. (p. 53)

All of which confirms that PACE was correct to see the Appropriate Adult as having the central role in the protection of the suspect's rights. It means, of course, that Appropriate Adults must know what is required of them and be able to resist pressure from numerous quarters. In general terms, the Appropriate Adult must act in ways similar to that of an interpreter, that is, to explain procedures, ensure that the police act properly, and minimise the risk of unreliable evidence. The Appropriate Adult is not part of a treatment programme – although too often seen as such by treatment agencies – nor required to offer legal assistance to anyone other than the suspect. The task of the Appropriate Adult is to protect the rights of suspects; to move beyond that is to distort the role.

Conclusion

There are clearly many more questions needing attention which have not been discussed. For example, should the Appropriate Adult sit in on any other interviews, including those with the psychiatrists, or probation officers, and if not, why not? Should the Appropriate Adult be given the same form of privilege granted to lawyers in order to prevent any repetition of that which occurred in the Rosemary West case? Should the Appropriate Adult be excluded from being a witness for the prosecution, being available only as witness for the defence?

These are important, but we need to tackle the basic problems first; that is, the actions of the custody officers, their decisions to call an Appropriate Adult, the duties of the Appropriate Adult once in the station, and who the Appropriate Adult should be. These are the important ones, others must wait.

In spite of these unanswered questions, and the confusion, ambiguities and difficulties surrounding the Appropriate Adult, he or she remains a useful means of protection for mentally disordered suspects. We ought not to believe this is a panacea for all the ills that mentally disordered suspects are heir to, for miscarriages of justice may still occur. But we have to believe that the Appropriate Adult is the best system there is, and its failings are as much political as jurisprudential. Without the political will to refine the concept, and require the police to use the Appropriate Adult more readily, local schemes, such as exist, will flounder. That would not be in the interests of the mentally disordered.

7

Diversion: its Place in the Scheme of Things

Diversion operates at the point where decisions can be made about whether a patient should or should not enter or remain in the criminal justice system. It does not fit easily into the current thrust towards community safety, for the aim is to treat rather than control or punish, and I say this without entering that debate about whether treatment is control or punishment. Perhaps the explanation lies in the differences between the various pressure groups; those wanting community safety are primarily concerned with controlling patients in the community, those for diversion are likely to be those supporting psychiatric values, and with a dislike of the criminal justice system. It is interesting that, over the years, supporters for diversion have had a considerable impact on policy, resulting in a government view that diversion should be pursued. As far as this book is concerned, and the central themes being followed therein, diversion needs to be examined sceptically to determine how, if at all, it helps to promote the integrity of mental health systems, and whether it fosters or frustrates community safety.

We can begin with an assertion: diversion has acquired something of a cult position, its supporters being almost evangelical in their enthusiasm, perhaps seeing it as a means by which offenders can be extracted from the jaws of the uncaring penal system (Cavadino 1999). Herschel Prins (1994, p. 146) adopts a more cautious stance, suggesting that those espousing diversion should be more critical. He says it is all too easy to assume that offenders wish to be diverted, yet for some diversion may reduce their sense of personal responsibility and produce an adverse outcome (ibid. p. 146). He has not always been listened to. There is in Britain a powerful anti-criminal justice lobby, which is highly suspicious of the criminal justice system, and diversion becomes a means of expressing that discontent.

Herschel Prins (1994) also notes that diversion is not new, having a long if somewhat obscure history going back at least to Henry VIII and probably earlier. Traditionally, diversion offered some protection to the mentally disordered from the customary consequences of their wrongdoing (ibid. p. 137), or, put in the modern idiom, an offender who is mentally disordered should be the subject of positive discrimination compared with others who are not so affected. Positive discrimination could take various forms. It could allow the Crown Prosecution Service (CPS) to discontinue a case 'where the CPS is satisfied that the probable effect upon the defendants' mental health outweighs the interests of justice in that particular case' (quoted in ibid. p. 142). It could allow the police not to proceed with the charge and divert the offender into the psychiatric services, or wherever else thought to be appropriate. It could allow offenders who are sentenced to be transferred out of the penal system into the psychiatric services and on occasions be transferred back if successful treatment occurs, that is, before the sentence is served.

Diversion schemes generally

Home Office Circular 66/90 (Home Office 1990) sets out government policy for dealing with mentally disordered offenders as it relates to diversion:

> It is Government policy that, wherever possible mentally disordered persons should receive care and treatment from the health and social services. Where there is insufficient evidence... that a mentally disordered person has committed an offence, careful consideration should be given to whether prosecution is required in the public interest. It is desirable that alternatives to prosecution, such as cautioning by the police and/or admission to hospital... should be considered first before deciding that prosecution is necessary. (para. 2)

We can take 'in the public interest' to mean where serious offences have been committed, so presumably those offenders committing the less serious offences can be dealt with by diversion.

> The Government recognises that this policy can be effective only if the courts and criminal justice agencies have access to health and social services. (ibid. para. 2)

There are two main routes by which offenders can be diverted out of the criminal justice system. First, by the police and courts using criminal justice powers, and second, through the powers of the 1983 Mental Health Act. In the first the following apply:

1(a)   For the police to take no further action or to caution formally the offender.
1(b)   For the Crown Prosecution Service to choose not to prosecute or to discontinue a prosecution.
1(c)   For the courts to use these powers to give bail (or make non-custodial penalties – but this is not strictly speaking diversion yet is often included as such).
1(d)   For the courts and others to use powers under bail and arrest referral schemes.

In the second, that is, through the Mental Health Act 1983, there are the following routes, although for these purposes they will not be considered in this chapter as most are dealt with elsewhere in this volume. They are included in order to set out the full range of possibilities.

2(a)   By the use of Section 136 of the 1983 Act which gives powers to remove a mentally disordered person to a place of safety, which could include a hospital.
2(b)   By the civil powers under the 1983 Act whereby an offender can be assessed by a psychiatrist and social worker as requiring compulsory admission to hospital.
2(c)   By the courts, who on receipt of psychiatric advice may remand a person to hospital for assessment or treatment, and the courts can dispose of the case by way of a hospital or guardianship order.
2(d)   By transferring an offender already in custody from prison to hospital.

In practice, these categories are not discrete. An offender may be brought to the police station on a Section 136 order but then charged with an offence (usually one against public order) if the police are unable to find suitable care elsewhere. Or as in 2(b) above, an offender may be charged with an offence, but after being seen by a psychiatrist and social worker is compulsorily admitted to a mental hospital under the civil powers contained in Sections 2 or 3 of the 1983 Mental Health Act, in which case no further action will be taken by the police.

Many of the largest and most important diversion schemes involve the police, who may divert offenders even before they are taken to the police station. These forms of diversion are more commonly referred to as cautions, of which there are two main types, the informal and the formal.

First, the informal caution, where the right of a constable to take no action against certain types of offenders is held under common law, and can be asserted even against the wishes of his chief constable (who is also a constable). Most of us have been subject to this informal caution at one time or another, usually for minor motoring offences. There are no data on the numbers of informal cautions issued annually or for individual police forces. Helen Jones (1992) makes the point that, if the person cautioned is mentally disordered, this strategy offers no health care, and, if the person is homeless, it simply puts him or her back on the streets. She adds that the police have no duty to look at the community care needs of such an individual, and little time or expertise to do anything on an informal basis (p. 12). Informal cautions do little to change the offender's plight, status or whatever, nor are they intended to.

Formal cautions are different. In England and Wales the police may formally caution an arrested offender – the procedure is not used in Scotland. Cautioning is essentially an administrative act based on the discretion of the police and has no statutory recognition. Home Office Cautioning Guidelines are contained in Circular 59/90 and 66/90 (para. 4(iii) quoted in Home Office 1994), but Local Force Policies Standing Orders are just as important. For example, the cautioning rates of the 43 police forces in England and Wales in 1992 for drug offences varied widely, ranging from 16% in West Yorkshire to 77% in Kent, where the differences can be explained by the policies of the local police who act according to local conditions (Home Office 1994). Formal cautioning has three main objectives:

1   To deal quickly and simply with less serious offences.
2   To divert them from the courts and thereby reduce the burden on the criminal justice system.
3   To reduce the chances of reoffending. (Home Office Circular 59/90, quoted in Home Office 1994)

Three conditions must be met before a caution can be administered. They are:

1   There must be evidence of the offender's guilt sufficient to give a realistic prospect of conviction.
2   The offender must admit the offence.

3   The offender (or in the case of a juvenile his parents or guardian) must understand the significance of a caution and give consent to being cautioned. (para. 4(iii) quoted in Home Office 1994)

When the first two conditions are met, the police officer concerned is required to consider the nature of the offence, the likely sentence, the offender's age, previous criminal history, attitude to the offence, the views of the victim, and the state of the offender's physical or mental health before issuing a caution (ibid. p. 49).

Home Office Circular 66/90 (Home Office 1990) sets out government policy for the two types of caution. For the informal one, it states:

> if the criteria for a caution (formal) are not met the police should consider whether any action needs to be taken against the suspect. In some cases the public interest might be met by diverting mentally disordered persons from the criminal justice system and finding alternatives to prosecution such as admission to hospital under Section 2 or 3 or to Guardianship under Section 7 of the 1983 Act or informal support in the community by Social Services Departments. (para. 4(iii))

For the formal cautions, it states:

> where it is suspected that a mentally disordered person may have committed an offence, consideration should be given – in consultation with the Crown Prosecution Service where appropriate – to whether any formal action by the police is necessary, particularly where it appears that prosecution is not required in the public interest in view of the nature of the offence. If the suspect is able to meet the requirements for a caution to be administered he might be cautioned. (para. 4 (iii))

Cautions offer the most likely opportunity for future development, for cautions operate at the point at which treatment for the mentally disordered can be provided. Some agencies talk 'of the need to find a solution to the problem of people with mental health problems being prosecuted inappropriately' (MIND 1993), but that avoids the difficult question, which is, diverted to what?

Diversion through the Crown Prosecution Service

Section 23(3) of the Prosecution of Offences Act 1985 provides the CPS with the power to discontinue criminal proceedings where this would be in the public interest. The Code for Crown Prosecutors (8(v)) endorses the spirit and objectives of Home Office Circular 66/90, so that:

> where there is evidence to establish that an accused person under investigation was suffering from mental disorder at the time the offence was committed, the Crown Prosecution will observe the principle that prosecution will not be appropriate in the circumstances, unless it is over ridden by the wider public interest, including in particular the gravity of the offence. (Code for Crown Prosecutors quoted in Bynoe 1993, p. 31)

The power to discontinue under Section 23 is available only during the early stages of the case in a Magistrates Court and must be effected before the trial, or before committal to a Crown Court (NACRO 1993, p. 10). The Code also draws attention to the possibility of obtaining a medical report, when the strain of criminal proceedings may lead to a worsening of the accused's mental health – noting that sometimes there may be additional strain due to the discovery of the offence, and that the accused's mental state will be relevant in considering any later issue of *mens rea* or unfitness to plead. Information from reports, including those by probation officers, may prompt the use of discontinuance. Powers given to the CPS to terminate proceedings are either under an application to the court to withdraw the case, or to offer no evidence and invite the court to acquit or discharge the defendant.

It is important that the CPS works with other agencies and collaborates with them. The CPS is highly dependent on the police, probation, psychiatric services and so on for information, particularly when the offender is being offered psychiatric treatment. For example, a psychiatrist may want to recommend to the court that an offender be dealt with in the Magistrates Court in order to allow a Hospital Order to be made. (That raises questions as to whether the CPS should discontinue proceedings altogether, and whether a conviction should remain on the offender's record. That decision must be made 'in the public interest' – the CPS may want the conviction to stand if the offence involves violence.) Or the police or probation service may want to suggest a particular outcome, given the offender's mental condition. The CPS should know this, and a key feature of recent CPS policy has been an interest in working together with other agencies to improve practice. It is now formally stated in the influential Home Office Circular 66/90 (1990) which states:

the development of effective liaison with health and social service authorities will play an essential role in developing satisfactory arrangements to respond constructively in such cases. (para 4(iii))

There are no available figures on the numbers or types of offender (or offence) where the CPS used their powers. A diversion scheme in Clerkenwell, London, which involved 201 referrals to a psychiatrist led to 58 (29%) of the cases being discontinued (Joseph 1992). The figure was likely to be higher than otherwise, as the Clerkenwell scheme involved more contact with the CPS than would be expected – normally one would expect about 4.6% of the cases to be diverted.

> The availability of a psychiatrist giving evidence in court not only provided the CPS with information about the defendant but also enabled them to ask questions and seek clarification of medical issues with which they were sometimes unfamiliar. The dialogue was important in giving the CPS confidence to consider discontinuing cases. It is virtually unknown for psychiatrists assessing defendants at prison to recommend the discontinuance of a case on public interest grounds. (Joseph 1992, p. 21)

The last sentence is interesting. One wonders why the psychiatric services rarely pass information to the CPS. As NACRO point out, probation officers can and often do pass on information in the expectation that the CPS might discontinue the prosecution, so why not the psychiatrists (NACRO 1994, p. 11)?

It is difficult to know how to assess the role of the CPS in the overall scheme of things. Some critics see diversion as another excuse for the CPS to use their power to discontinue – in a study of Leicester Magistrates Court, over 40% of all cases were discontinued (Bean 1998). Critics adopting a less sardonic view see the role of the CPS as crucial but underused. The Reed Report (Department of Health 1992b) noted the priority given to dealing with mentally disordered offenders in the *Health of the Nation* (Department of Health 1992a) which said:

> The essential task here is to ensure that mentally disordered offenders who need specialist help and social care are diverted from the criminal justice system as early as possible. This requires close co-operation between all the agencies concerned.

If diversion is to be a feature of government policy, then the CPS have an important part to play. The question is how best to perform that role? There are many possibilities: one of which is to expect greater cooperation from other agencies, including the police and the police surgeons, who could inform them of their assessments; another is to clarify their own position, so that other agencies know what to expect of them.

Diversion through the courts

There are no statutory provisions for courts to divert offenders; the provision under which the courts can use diversion was intended otherwise, that is, for adjournments and remands. Adjournments allow the offender to be diverted out of the criminal justice system more easily, whereas remands retain the offender within the system, that is, they take place in order that a decision can be made for sentence or for trial. Consecutive or continuous adjournments are not permitted.

An adjournment *sine die* by the Magistrates Court allows the case to be reopened if required, although in practice this rarely occurs. Remands usually involve relatively short periods, either in custody or on bail, where the aim is to obtain more information, usually through a psychiatric report and/or a probation report. Decisions can then be made, which could lead to a *sine die* adjournment, or a sentence of which psychiatric treatment forms a part, that is, a Probation Order with a condition of treatment, or a Hospital Order. (These sentences are sometimes mistakenly seen as diversions but they do not involve the offenders being diverted out of the criminal justice system.) Remands and adjournments become closely interwoven (for a discussion on many of the legal issues involved, including the power of the court to remand to hospital and to impose an interim Hospital Order, see Fennell 1991).

Treatment may be as an inpatient or as an outpatient during an adjournment or remand, although if the offender fails to report, or fails to keep appointments, it is unlikely the magistrates will continue their support (James 1996, p. 23). The range of facilities, and the types of scheme being offered are wide: Blumenthal and Wessely (1992), in their survey of diversion schemes based in Magistrates Courts in England and Wales, found some operated on the initiative of an individual psychiatrist who attended court, and others involved participating agencies – these may also involve a panel scheme. Psychiatric assessment schemes were thought to have more to do with the availability of local forensic services than local needs (ibid. p. 1324). One of the most widely registered, the Clerkenwell scheme in central London, was aimed at reducing the frequency and length of custodial medical remands by providing a psychiatric assessment at the Magistrates Court. The conclusion was that the scheme was successful; it reduced the length of time spent in custody, and, more importantly, in some cases avoided custody altogether. For those acutely psychotic defendants who were admitted directly to hospital, it avoided a potentially lengthy, distressing remand (Joseph and Potter 1990).

Bail and arrest referral schemes

The fourth category is a catch-all group. Where an offender requires assessment or treatment, then early investigation of the options by way of bail can be of assistance. Bail schemes are usually administered by the probation service, which may involve the services of a consultant psychiatrist. The accommodation is usually in local bail hostels – the West Midlands Probation Service in Birmingham has one such hostel. If the offender is on police bail, the police may choose not to prosecute if the offender is being successfully diverted – sometimes the police will refer to the CPS for advice (NACRO 1993, p. 15).

There are various types of arrest referral schemes, some of which may involve nothing more than supplying the offender with an address to seek assistance or accommodation, others involve treatment agencies, attending the police station and offering advice on treatment. Others offer incentives contingent on receiving treatment. There is no information on the number of such schemes or on their effectiveness.

Mentally disordered in prison

The position of the mentally disordered in prison raises different questions as far as diversion is concerned. Diversion in this context involves prisoners being diverted out of the prison system to more favourable institutions so that they can receive appropriate treatment and care. The prison service lacks the facilities to treat serious conditions, psychiatric or otherwise. Why then could not prisons be brought up to the level where they are able to undertake that treatment? Behind that apparently innocuous question lies minefield after minefield where accusation and counter-accusation are rife, and where answers are still not forthcoming.

We can begin by noting a Report of the Joint Prison Service and National Health Service Executive Working Group in March 1999, which considered the future organisation of, and ways of improving, prisoners' health care, including their mental health. The Report addressed the question of establishing more formal links, at all levels, so that

> the care of mentally ill prisoners should develop in line with NHS mental health policy including new arrangements for referral and admission to high and medium secure psychiatric services. (Department of Health 1999a)

Linking the prison service to the NHS has been the driving force in the current debate, how much further this can go is the unanswered question.

I am not concerned here with the general problems of prisoners' health care, although of course that impinges on all else, including diversion. I want, however, to concentrate on diversion. In 1991, a Report of the Prison Advisory Group (Department of Health/Home Office 1991) noted that it is striking that, while there is a clear policy for diverting and/or transferring mentally disordered offenders from custody, there is no equivalent policy statement covering the care and treatment of those in need of mental health care who remain in prison (p. 13). The prison service continues to deal with many mentally disordered prisoners, in spite of the government's policy on diversion. For example, the remand population contains a heavy burden of mentally disordered prisoners – estimated at a rate 15 times higher than would be expected in the general population – almost certainly because the courts remand mentally disordered offenders in custody to receive treatment, rather than for matters of public safety or seriousness of offence (Grounds 1991). The Prison Advisory Group (op. cit. 1991, p. 5) said 'in principle it is wrong that courts should be able to remand to prison for the primary purpose of medical assessment' and sought changes to the bail statutes and regulations to make the changes.

Studies of the sentenced population show high rates of psychiatric morbidity (Gunn et al. 1991), although not as high as the remand group. It is estimated that more than 1 in 3 of the adult male population were psychiatrically disturbed, about 15,000 prisoners in England and Wales, while over 3% of prisoners, about 1,100, were so seriously affected as to require immediate hospital treatment. Most of these were suffering from schizophrenia or other forms of psychotic illness.

There are provisions for those serving a sentence of imprisonment, and those on remand, to be transferred (diverted) to hospital by warrant under a direction from the Home Secretary under Sections

47(i) and 48 of the 1983 Mental Health Act, if he is satisfied, having regard to the public interest, that it is expedient to do so. There must be reports from at least two medical practitioners stating *inter alia* that treatment is likely to alleviate or prevent a deterioration of his condition. If treatment is successful, then, before the earliest date of release, the patient can be returned to prison to complete the sentence, or to appear at court if unsentenced. About 1,000 such directives occur annually – a steady increase over the past decade. It is also usual for the Home Secretary to impose a restriction directive under Section 49 for any prisoner transferred to hospital.

To return to the question asked above: why are transfers needed? The legal answer is that prisons do not have the facilities or the powers to treat mentally disordered offenders without consent under Sections 2 or 3 of the 1983 Act. Prisons are not 'hospitals' within the meaning of the Mental Health Act. That is to say, prisoners may refuse medication, except in a *bona fide* emergency, where treatments can be given under common law, and, apart from this, treatment cannot be given in prison against the prisoners wishes within the provisions of the Mental Health Act 1983. Whether they could be or whether they should be are equally important questions needing consideration.

There is, of course, a straightforward practical problem. While all prisons must have medical facilities, some have no full-time medical officer and many have no full-time psychiatrist. Those that do may still not have the necessary facilities to deal with patients with the more florid mental disorders, or those with chronic conditions. Currently, transfers to outside hospitals are necessary, in the same way that transfers to hospital from prison for certain somatic conditions are also necessary, and for the same reasons, that is, that they cannot be dealt with inside the prison. The Prison Advisory Group put it this way:

> Although the position varies between prisons, in general there is little specific provision for offenders with mental health care needs beyond that provided by visiting psychiatrists in order to provide assessments and reports for court etc. – a task which is shared with full time prison medical officers who do not always have recognised psychiatric qualifications. (op. cit. pp. 22–3)

Transferring mentally disordered prisoners to a hospital where they can be treated is anything but straightforward. A report on mentally disordered remand prisoners comments that the criterion in Section 48 of the 1983 Act that a prisoner requires 'urgent' treatment is interpreted unduly narrowly (Dell et al. quoted in ibid. p. 8), which in part explains the discrepancy between the numbers of prisoners diagnosed as mentally disordered and those transferred. There are also delays in obtaining assessments of prisoners from consultants, as well as problems identifying the appropriate catchment area hospital – the average interval in British prisons between being admitted to prison and the visit by an outside physician was about four weeks (ibid. p. 10). This is in spite of accusations about the manner in which the prison service deals with these patients. For example, Dr Herridge (1989), in a letter to the *Psychiatric Bulletin*, says prisoners in Brixton prison are housed in special medical rooms which 'are bare apart for a mattress, extremely dirty... [and] patients are often naked because of their mental condition, and have only a canvas blanket to keep them warm' (p. 200). His solution is an emergency treatment order of three days duration to be made by a Section 12(2) doctor on the prison medical staff, which, he believes, 'would enable treatment to begin and the patient housed under more acceptable conditions. It would also allow time to seek help from the catchment psychiatric hospital or the Regional Secure Unit' (ibid. p. 201). Whether that would ease the problem is not clear; it might encourage further delays if the outside consultant knew that treatment was being given, and may make it more difficult for the outside consultant to assess accurately the patient's condition.

Then there is the reluctance on behalf of psychiatric institutions such as regional secure units to take these prisoners, especially if violent or likely to be disruptive to the existing ward atmosphere. Nursing staff naturally will not welcome violent patients, and, whether violent or not, these patients demand, and often receive, a disproportionate level of psychiatric time. Existing acute services are already stretched, and other patients, not offenders, may be regarded as more deserving.

Making all prison hospitals into 'hospitals' within the meaning of the 1983 Mental Health Act and permiting prisoners to be sectioned and given compulsory treatment appears, on the face of it, sensible and obvious. Attractive though it may be, it meets with considerable opposition from the prison medical service staff. The objections vary, some are trivial, some not so. At the trivial end is an element of distrust between the services, for example the Prison Advisory Group listed numerous complaints that NHS consultants had in obtaining access to prisoners, even before undertaking assessments of them. These included the inflexibility of the prison regime, which prevents appointments being made at the beginning or end of the working day, or at lunchtime or at weekends. Neither was the prison environment seen as conducive to carrying out psychiatric assessments, as the assessment facilities were poor, and medical records were sometimes withheld from visiting psychiatrists (Department of Health/Home Office, 1991, p. 11).

Trivial though these may appear to outsiders, within the prison system small obstacles build up to large ones, and trivia takes on an insurmountable dimension. The complaints, however, illustrate an underlying tension between the outside NHS services and the prison medical service. That tension shows itself when NHS consultants refer to the prison medical service in less than complimentary terms, and where the prison medical service is seen as employing lower status physicians. The prison medical service has for many years resisted attempts to be incorporated into the NHS, claiming to have developed a measure of expertise alongside a special understanding of prisons and prisoners, which they say comes from their unique medical experience within the prison system. The Fallon Report (Department of Health 1999b) referred obliquely to these tensions and asked, 'Could not the Prison Service attract more therapists of whatever discipline to work within the penal system?' The answer, it said, was probably no, and added somewhat revealingly, 'Throughout its history the prison medical service has struggled, without much success, to attract high quality medical, nursing and other clinical staff' (para. 1.35.17).

An alternative approach has been for the NHS to take over responsibility for medical services within prisons 'lock, stock and barrel' (ibid.). The Fallon Report was clear: 'We recommend that the NHS takes over responsibility for healthcare within prisons' (Department of Health 1999b, Recommendation 48, p. 402). This is easier said than done, and takes no account of the logistical problems involved. Small prisons, with a local GP acting as part-time medical officer, with no psychiatric training, could not expect to have their equally small hospital wing elevated to a hospital within the meaning of the Act. But what of large prisons? Could they not be developed to deal with psychiatric patients; this may help to avoid transfers for all but the chronic long stay? The answer is, probably yes.

Critics say such facilities will encourage the courts to send more mentally disordered offenders to prison, that being a guarantee of treatment, and that such a development would shift the focus of the prison from a detaining, punitive institution to one that is treatment orientated. Also, they say it would depart from the traditional view of prison; treatment has never been its main role, it being more orientated to punishment with a strong retributive and utilitarian flavour. Moreover, such changes require legislation to take away the prisoner's powers of consent, and to do so would grant the prison even more power over the inmates than before.

There *is* a danger that courts would send more offenders who were mentally disordered to prison and this must be addressed, preferably by legislation. However, treating offenders in prison would not change the role of prison, rather it would reinforce its position as the institution dealing with offenders irrespective of their medical/psychiatric condition. The Fallon Report talked of a need for a short-term mechanism for resolving disagreements between the prison service and the NHS, but wanted 'a truly integrated high quality service across the whole range of forensic services' (Department of Health 1999b, para. 7.3.19, p. 402). That, if it were to be implemented, would be for the long term.

The immediate short-term problem is how best to improve existing services in a selected number of large prisons. There is, I think, much in the proposal suggested above which is valuable especially where the aim is to designate a selected few as hospitals within the meaning of the Act, then evaluate them and, if satisfactory, move ahead cautiously. Provisions will still be required to transfer some prisoners until facilities improve. This step-by-step approach is similar to that proposed by the Prison Advisory Group who wanted priority to be given to the development of services for remand prisoners. It also noted that there needs to be a coherent policy on the range of treatment services provided, on the selection of prisoners to receive treatment and on the flexibility in moving prisoners between treatment establishments according to their needs (Department of Health/Home Office 1991, para. 5.24).

It also noted the other tricky problem of accreditation, where the relevant professional bodies must formally accredit the work in the prison as part of a recognised training package in psychiatry. All are important but all could be resolved with the will to make the necessary changes; the warning from the Advisory Group, however, should not be ignored. It said that examples of special provisions are not typical of the services for prisoners with mental health care needs. Few specific provisions exist beyond that provided by visiting psychiatrists in order to provide assessments and reports for courts (ibid. para. 5.25); the new proposals would require different staffing arrangements to that usually occurring within the prison, with a consultant psychiatrist leading the team. That is not likely to be welcomed by the prison medical service, where contracting in specialist psychiatric care reduces their status and devalues their claim to expertise.

Effectiveness of diversion

In spite of the enthusiasm in some quarters for diversion, it is difficult to find much reported success – 'success' for these purposes does not include the prison service. Definitions of success vary: to some, success means according to the numbers taken out of the criminal justice system for the 'aim of diversion is to reduce the role of the criminal justice system and increase that of the health service' (Blumenthal and Wessely 1992, p. 1322). For others, it is about reductions in the length of the remand period (Joseph and Potter 1990), or it is drawing attention to the plight of the mentally disordered, to provide 'a broader multi-agency focus, which of itself can make disposals easier' (Department of Health 1992b, para. 6). While for others 'The task is not diversion. The task is to centre on the needs of this group of people. Diversion is simply one way to access this task' (James 1996, p. 23).

The range of personnel involved further complicates matters. Some schemes use a psychiatrist, others a community nurse, some are probation projects where the probation officer advises the CPS (as in the Public Interest Case Assessment scheme review in inner London) and some use a multidisciplinary panel. In her review of diversion schemes, Ann James concludes 'that we know a lot about the diversion process and about diversion schemes. How they work, how to set them up [but] measures of effectiveness are harder to come by' (ibid. p. 22).

If the effectiveness of diversion is measured in terms of numbers transferred out of the criminal justice system, then diversion can be said to work. Numerous reports suggest large numbers are transferred, usually through police cautions, or through the CPS where the case is discontinued (see ibid.). Schemes involving the police seem to be the most successful, if only because they are the least complicated, involving the decision of one person, the custody officer. They tend, however, to divert low-level offenders: for example, Cooke (1991) in Glasgow found the diverted offenders were unusual in that most were first-time offenders, they had less serious offending histories, with a large proportion of female offenders. In contrast, the Clerkenwell scheme, which was court based, had offenders with high rates of previous psychiatric contact, where 77% had previous convictions (James and Hamilton 1991).

Transferring offenders out of the system can only be one of a number of aims, and these must be set against others such as public protection, a reduction in homelessness, and so on. Moreover, diversion is only as effective as the services to which it diverts. Too often, the suspicion is that appropriate services are not available, so that the offender is sent out expecting to receive treatment where no treatment exists; the offender is then simply recycled to reappear in court for another set of offences. A key aim of diversion is to reduce criminality, but again few data are available, so that we do not know whether diversion schemes reduce offending, delay it or have no impact at all.

These, if nothing else, should temper some of the enthusiasm of those who appear to accept diversion uncritically. The stance adopted by Herschel Prins (1994, p. 146) seems the correct one; it *is* too easy to assume that offenders wish to be diverted, yet for some diversion may reduce their sense of responsibility and produce an adverse outcome. Under diversion, the offender and the public do not always receive the protection they deserve. McKettrick and Eysenck (quoted in Cooke 1991, pp. 789–91) say 'the public interest, the rights of the victims, are not seen as relevant to their decision making'. Schemes are often much too offender orientated, yet paradoxically 'automatically deprive him of the benefit of legal advice' (ibid.). The Ritchie Report on the Clunis enquiry wanted diversion to apply only to those committing minor offences, and encouraged victims to prosecute serious offenders who are diverted out of the criminal justice system.

> It seems to us a matter of real concern that a mental patient's serious crimes are overlooked, often because the victim is not willing to prosecute, probably he knows the assailant is mentally ill. We agree that it is right to keep the mentally ill away from the criminal justice system for minor offences. But it seems wrong to us that a person who is mentally ill should not be prosecuted for a serious offence and should thereby be deprived of the real help they might otherwise receive under a Hospital Order or the Probation Service. We consider that the police should encourage the victim to prosecute in such cases. (Ritchie et al. 1994)

That is to say, positive discrimination for the mentally disordered should be reserved for low-level offenders. Even then and returning to Herschel Prins' point, offenders may not always have their rights respected under diversion. Offenders can easily be placed under pressure to admit to the offence in order to participate in treatment, when a legal advisor would see a defence to the allegations (in Cooke op. cit.). Admitting guilt might mean having the charge dropped, but it may also mean that the police will receive information they may not have received otherwise, and record a conviction which would not be recorded otherwise.

Cooperation between agencies

Much has been said about the need for agency cooperation; diversion and cooperation are but two names for the same activity, as diversion can only exist if there are available services to which the offender can be diverted. NACRO (1994, p. 14) regard the 'greatest obstacle to increasing the effectiveness of diversion as the complex separation of powers and responsibilities across the health, social services and criminal justice system'. The problem, NACRO says, is made worse because there is no key agency able to take the lead or be responsible for promoting diversion: the police and probation service have a limited part to play, where the police are only involved up to the trial, and the probation service is not involved until prosecution (ibid.). In the circumstances, one would have thought that agencies would work together but sadly cooperation occurs all too infrequently.

It is axiomatic that the decarceration movement, which has reduced the number of hospital beds (from about 175,000 in 1975 to about 51,000 in 1992) was *inter alia* a response to fiscal pressures and a retrenchment of welfare policies. It is very doubtful if it was a movement which grew out of a specific concern for the patients' welfare. Community responses are not cheap and certainly not cheaper than institutional care, and the facilities provided are not necessarily more humane – accusations of dumping mental patients to be neglected or exploited are common. The penal services, including the police, welcome diversion, for they have most to gain; however, it gets hard to place an offender out of the system. It does not mean that the receiving psychiatric services will be equally welcoming; the talk may be of diversion but the practical reality is often different.

NACRO (1993), which has introduced a number of diversion schemes, give numerous examples where the existing services failed to cooperate, whether with each other or with the criminal justice system. Some of the difficulties were due to a lack of resources, where agencies found themselves unable to take in extra work; others were due to the lack of shared information between them, which was said to be 'limited and uncoordinated' (p. 22). Requests for FMEs, ASWs and psychiatrists to attend police stations often led to delays, for sometimes these professionals failed to attend, or did so at different times, resulting in lost opportunities to divert (ibid. p. 22).

Whether the NACRO findings are typical is not known, but they come as no surprise, given what we know about interagency cooperation generally. After all, why should agencies cooperate? On the face of it there is little advantage for them. They must take on extra work, and are already underresourced and overflowing with potential cases. NACRO concluded that 'establishing and operating inter agency projects of this kind is not easy or straightforward in practice' (ibid.). NACRO insisted that the schemes had worked, but did not say how or in what way. Many agencies found that operating these diversion schemes was the first time that they had been required to collaborate. They pointed out that difficulties needed to be overcome in establishing interagency cooperation.

There have been additional complications with purchaser/provider systems in the health service, at least up to 1999. Purchaser/provider is defined as the process by which needs are identified and services are required to respond to those needs which are specified, paid for and monitored. To those not familiar with those purchasing/providing systems, the whole matter seems immediately unintelligible, with its management jargon, its assumption that 'needs' are known or definable, and its emphasis on contracts and all that goes with that. Purchasing services for offenders with mental disorders was regarded as 'an advanced task in the basic field of purchasing mental health services and care in the community and success is unlikely unless these are done well' (Charlewood and Fender 1993, p. 16).

Under the purchaser/provider system, the job was done, or not done, according to the way the health services divided up their work. Its contracts were usually of a general nature, which involved purchasing services from a range of agencies, but occasionally they might be more specific, involving the purchase of one type of service, or they might only include provision for service assessment. Under that system, all kinds of problems could have arisen. For example, if the health authority had not purchased services to deal with offenders in police stations, then no psychiatric services would be available for a Section 136 assessment. In which case, the police would have had to call the patient's own GP, or contact some other service provider. It was possible, although unlikely, that contracts would have been couched in such as way as to exclude police stations, or exclude offenders who lived or were domiciled outside the catchment area. If the police station was excluded, then the FME would have had to take the offender to the local hospital casualty department to receive the necessary treatment.

I mention these possibilities because the old purchaser/provider systems could distort or dislocate local diversion schemes. Things have changed a little; there is more flexibility in the system where the old system has been replaced by commissioning arrangements (NHS Confederation 1999). Certain types of service are to be subject to specialist commissioning at a local level. A health authority may take the lead in commissioning services which could include high security commissioning, the aim being to permit offenders to be able to move more freely throughout the system. There is in addition the National Service Framework (NSF), which is one of a series of frameworks for key specialisms which represent a core part of the modernisation programme for the NHS and for mental health services. 'The first priority is services for people with severe and enduring mental illness' (Sainsbury Centre for Mental Health 1999). Although milestones are not set beyond 2002, the official Introduction to the NSF says that 'implementing the NSF fully across the NHS and social services, and throughout other agencies could take up to 10 years'.

Clearly, services for the mentally disordered are a top priority for the NHS in the next decade. We must hope that they will be realised. Hopefully, the NHS will be able to provide that whole range of services for the mentally disordered, whether offender or not, in a way that removes some of the anomalies in the earlier system and reduces some of the expectations placed on diversion.

Conclusion

Support for diversion comes from varying organisations, not least the government and the influential Reed Report (Department of Health 1992b). The widely quoted Home Office Circular 66/90 set the scene in drawing attention to the services responsible for dealing with the mentally disordered offender 'in relation to existing legal powers' and

> the desirability of ensuring effective co-operation between agencies to ensure the best use is made of resources, and that mentally disordered persons are not prosecuted when this is not required by the public interest. (Home Office 1990)

The Reed Report picked this up. It adopted the same principles as Circular 66/90 above, wherein the government reaffirmed that mentally disordered offenders should receive care and treatment from health and social services rather than the criminal justice system.

It is difficult to see how much more we can expect from diversion. Without agency cooperation and without a fundamental change in agency attitudes, it seems cooperation is unlikely to develop further. One wonders too about the wisdom of extending diversion further and positively discriminating against offenders with a mental disorder, for, as was said earlier, that may be a mixed blessing. Perhaps we have reached the point at which we begin to seek alternative ways of dealing with the mentally disordered, and the suggestion throughout this book is that we build up the psychiatric resources of the criminal justice system, at the same time as the NSF services develop. Of course, that will not deal with the countless numbers of offenders diverted by the police on formal and informal cautions, but neither should it. They can continue as before. It is the others that are of interest; those offenders who slip through the police net and turn up in the courts.

We can, however, expect more from the priority given to mentally disordered offenders by NHS Trusts. For the first time, the government has set out a comprehensive agenda for mental health services, which acknowledges that the whole system of mental health care must be made to work if we are to succeed in modernising care (Sainsbury Centre for Mental Health 1999). That at least is one step forward, so that perhaps diversion is seen to be less important.

8

Dual Diagnosis and Control

In this chapter, the aim is to look ahead and highlight some of the likely areas of difficulty facing those services dealing with the mentally disordered offender. Already some of the warning signs have appeared, so that it is less about predicting what is going to arrive, and more about assessing what has arrived and determining what can be done about it. A recent arrival and one likely to cast a long shadow in the immediate future is dual diagnosis.

Dual diagnosis changes things in ways not yet understood, if only because it produces new problems for the mental health services, and for all who work with the mentally disordered. In this chapter, I want to sketch out some of the essential features of dual diagnosis, more to act as a beacon than to connect to the main theme of the book. Dual diagnosis affects the mental health and drug treatment services in numerous ways: some likely to cause tensions, with others promoting demands for new forms of cooperation.

Dual diagnosis is a broad term indicating the simultaneous presence of two interdependent disorders – dual disorder is better but that too is misleading, as some patients can, and occasionally do, have more than two disorders, including perhaps HIV. Common examples of dual diagnosis include depression with cocaine use, alcohol addiction with panic reactions and personality disorder with episodic drug use (Ries 1994, p. 4). The disorders may vary along important dimensions such as severity, chronicity, durability and degree of impairment of functioning. They may be severe or mild, with one more severe than the other. Compared with patients with a single disorder, those with dual diagnosis often require longer periods of treatment, have more crises and progress more gradually in treatment (ibid. p. 4).

Whatever one may think of the problems posed by earlier patients, whether offenders or not, and whatever one may think of the quality of service provision, at least their plight was not complicated by a second disorder. Mental patients and drug users have traditionally remained apart: they have been treated in separate institutions by separate experts with very specific skills. The literature on their aetiology, diagnosis and treatment has remained separate, as has the legislation which governs them. Dual diagnosis brings them together, at least theoretically, whether it does so practically, that is, in terms of service provision, is another matter.

Alcohol and drug dependence are classified by the World Health Organization as mental disorders, but do not of themselves permit detention under the 1983 Mental Health Act. Section 1 of the 1983 Act makes it clear that:

> nothing in this Section shall be construed as implying that a person will be dealt with under the Act as suffering from mental disorder or from any form of mental disorder by reason only of promiscuity or other immoral conduct, social deviancy, or dependence on alcohol or drugs.

In the Draft Proposals in the Review of the 1983 Act (Richardson 1999), the Committee wanted this changed 'because the social context within which it was felt necessary has changed' (p. 19). However, in the subsequent *Review of the Mental Health Act 1983* (Department of Health 1999), the Committee changed its mind and opted to return to the status quo.

Before we look at that, I want first to look more closely at the nature of dual diagnosis, the origins of which can be found in the social upheavals of the 1960s and 70s. The decarceration movement emptied the mental hospitals, leaving many mentally disordered patients homeless and untreated. Coincidentally, the same period was characterised by an unprecedented growth in the use of illegal substances. Some of the mentally disordered became drug users, and some of the drug users became mentally disordered. That some drug users injected themselves with non-sterile needles and became HIV positive or contracted full-blown AIDS merely added to the problems. Comorbidity, which had hitherto been rare, was now becoming commonplace, although there was, and still is, a marked reluctance by health service professionals to admit to a problem. Too often drug users found themselves being dealt with under the Mental Health Act because their condition resembled or mimicked a mental disorder, while the mentally disordered found themselves classified as drug users for the same reason.

Some epidemiological data

Dual diagnosis is a term largely derived from America where it was recognised as a clinical condition going back at least to the early 1980s.

In Britain it remains largely unknown, being recognised and accepted only by a few specialist treatment units. There is little data in Britain from which to assess the extent of the problem, and little evidence to suggest that policies are being developed to deal with it. The American literature is more extensive. The most comprehensive study is the Epidemiological Catchment Area Study (ECAS), where 20,291 people were interviewed in research by the National Institute of Mental Health (NIMH) (Regier et al. 1990). The sampling procedure was complex, as was the interviewing schedule: the one used was the NIMH Diagnostic Interview, which is a highly structured schedule designed for large epidemiological studies. The methodological problems were immense, not least because it was necessary to account for and subsequently discount transient symptoms of mental disorder which occur during the withdrawal period of substance abuse, as well as in the acute intoxication stage. Hallucinations, along with high levels of anxiety, are common during these periods; accordingly these were not rated as mental disorders, if they were found only in the presence of alcohol or other drugs. (For a full account of the methodology see ibid.) Thus, the results overall tended to be of a conservative nature.

The results of the study show that among individuals with any lifetime mental disorder, 22.3% had a lifetime history of alcohol abuse/dependence, 14.7% had other drug abuse/dependence, and 28.9% of those had some other form of addictive disorder. This compares with those who had no history of mental disorder, where the rate for alcohol abuse/dependence was 11%, other drug abuse/dependence 3.7% and for the others it was 13.2%. Having a lifetime mental disorder suggests there is more than twice the risk of alcohol abuse/dependence and over four times the risk of having another drug abuse/dependence (14.7% compared with 3.7%) (ibid.).

In terms of specific mental disorders, the results are equally interesting. Of all individuals with a lifetime diagnosis of schizophrenia, that is, about 1.5% of the US population, 47.0% met the criteria for having some form of substance abuse, whereas for those with antisocial personality it was 83.6%, for anxiety disorders it was much lower at 14.6%, but for endogenous depression it was 32.0% and for manic depression it was higher again at 60.7%. Looked at from the opposite perspective, that is, from the point of view of substance abusers, the results show that of persons with a drug diagnosis, other than alcohol, 53.1% had a lifetime rate for mental disorder (ibid.).

The ECAS, with its large sample base, has been able to produce a unique set of results, unmatched anywhere. It also produces striking conclusions which should sound a clear warning to policy makers in the UK. The authors say:

> These data provide clear and persuasive evidence that mental disorder must be addressed as part of substance abuse prevention efforts... For mental health professionals it is also important to recognise the high rates of substance abuse disorders among those with severe mental disorder. (ibid. p. 2517)

There is no reason to believe that the position in Britain is different from the US. Levels of substance abuse are similar, and the decarceration movement, which involved emptying the large mental hospitals, has proceeded at a similar pace. The two conditions necessary for those high levels of comorbidity are present: the high levels of substance abuse and large numbers of mental patients in the community.

Not surprisingly, the British research is scanty and nowhere approaches that of the US. (Over 500 papers were found on dual diagnosis in the US whereas only 5 were found in Britain up to June 1999.) Two British studies are of interest. Matthews et al. (1991) studied 908 patients admitted to two London hospitals and found 13% tested positive for cannabis. Menezes et al. (1996) examined 171 patients diagnosed as psychotic in south London and found 31.6% were alcohol dependent and 15.8% tested positive for substance abuse. These results are lower than for the ECAS and may be due to a number of methodological differences, not least that the samples may be from atypical areas, taken as they were from two London boroughs. There is a need to establish prevalence rates on wider and more representative samples (Gournay et al. 1997).

Research in this area is fraught with methodological difficulties. Many of the early US studies failed to use a standardised instrument of diagnostic criteria making comparisons difficult. Much of the data are contaminated, although the ECAS avoided many of the more obvious pitfalls and was rigorous enough to exclude symptoms of mental disorder, if they were found only in the presence of alcohol or other drugs. Rates for age, sex and ethnicity need to be standardised – these are usually taken from the last census data which may well be three or four years old, and almost certainly out of date by the time the research is conducted.

There are also problems with the selection of the sample. Young people tend to have higher rates of substance abuse than the older group, so that a younger group of psychiatric patients will expect to show higher rates of substance abuse – in the US, patients over the age

of 45 years tended to have much lower rates of substance abuse, sometimes 50% lower. Men, generally speaking, are likely to have higher
rates of substance abuse than women – sometimes twice as high – and
blacks are likely to have higher rates than whites, again about twice as
high.

Then there is the problem about the sampling frame and from where
the sample is taken. The ECAS sampled from the community and institutions, taking adults aged 18 years and over. For the community
sample, one adult was interviewed from selected households, and from
institutions residents were taken from long-term mental hospitals,
nursing homes and penal institutions. These were sampled at higher
probability rates than the community population – this was to take
account of differences found in the various institutions (Regier et al.
1990). For example, the prevalence of substance abuse is known to vary
according to location, treatment setting and programme admission
criteria. Higher rates will be found in prisons, in hospital emergency
rooms – especially after midnight – and among homeless populations.
In contrast, those psychiatric services centring more on medical settings
will have lower rates of substance abuses. In spite of the care taken,
questions can be asked about whether the ECAS was methodologically
sound; the answer is likely to be a qualified yes; qualified because no
sampling frame is entirely free from methodological error, some, like
the ECAS, are simply better than others (Smith and Hucker 1994).

In addition, there is the problem of obtaining data, especially from
substance abusers. Underreporting information on any illicit activity,
but especially substance abuse, is a continuing methodological problem
which varies according to the population sampled. Young women with
small children will tend to underreport, fearing that information could
mean their children will be taken into care. Remand prisoners will also
underreport, being concerned about their sentence, so too will convicted
prisoners who are candidates for parole. There is no single reliable or
valid instrument available to overcome these problems; urine testing
provides an obvious test of validity but is neither practical nor possible
in studies involving large samples. Solutions, such as there are, must be
found in the quality of the interviewers, and the interviewers' ability to
convey trust and create confidence in the respondent.

To these methodological problems definitional problems need to be
added; what for example does substance abuse mean? Does it involve a
definition of abuse (as opposed to use), and should it include licit drugs
such as alcohol? What does mental disorder mean and are the symptoms
in dual diagnosis equivalent to other classes of mental disorder such as
depression?

Certainly, epidemiological studies are urgently needed in Britain. Coming rather late into this research area, we can take some lessons from the American experience. One, we need a large and comprehensive database, two, we need to agree on an operational definition that will allow comparability across a range of studies (Brown et al. 1989), and three, we need to obtain representative samples, with good self-report data on those engaged in illicit activities.

Comorbidity or aetiology?

In spite of what was said above, identifying dual diagnosis patients is relatively easy, the difficult part is establishing aetiology. Dual diagnosis is simply another form of comorbidity, itself meaning the presence of two disorders. More specifically, comorbidity means the presence of more than one specific disorder in a person over a defined period of time, usually at the same time but not necessarily so. The difficult bit is to determine whether there is a direct causal relationship between those two conditions, or whether they are separate and unrelated, that is, to what extent is comorbidity real or an artefact?

Those who see the relationships as real, argue that the presence of one often predisposes the other, that is, substance abuse leads to mental illness and mental illness leads to substance abuse. They cite the clinical and statistical evidence of examined comorbidities, which give a *prima facie* case for suggesting that a direct causal connection exists. Conversely, those supporting the latter remain unconvinced about the existing evidence, which they say claims a systemic relationship between disorders which remains unsubstantiated. They recognise the existence of comorbidities but say these could easily arise as a result of the methods of assessment, and of the help-seeking patterns of the population concerned. They point to the other possibility that the conditions are discrete with no connection at all. They are right to be sceptical, it being easy to slip into a way of thinking just because it appears convenient to do so, and it is right to challenge the research evidence, which is far from complete.

The debate about aetiology continues. Much research has been directed at the schizophrenic patient where, unfortunately, the results also remain equivocal – if anything, the more research that is undertaken, the more varied are the results and the more complex the issues. There remain disputes about the types of illegal drug used by schizophrenic patients, the impact of those drugs on the disease condition, whether they precede or follow the mental disorder and the extent and impact of alcohol use by these patients. In one particularly interesting British study (Bell 1965), a detailed examination was made of the nature and types of hallucination in schizophrenic patients. The hallucinations in drug-free schizophrenic patients were compared with a group of inpatients with an amphetamine psychosis. Differences occurred in the duration of the hallucinations; drug-induced hallucinations usually cleared up within 10 days of withdrawal from the drug, while schizophrenic hallucinations usually lasted longer. There were also differences in the quality of the hallucinations; visual images dominated in the drug-induced cases, but these were less common in the schizophrenic patients (Bell 1965 quoted in Turner and Tsuang 1990, p. 88).

There is also disagreement in the literature about which drugs are most abused by schizophrenic patients. Negrete et al. (1986) argue that 'Investigation of the co-occurrence of drug abuse and schizophrenia should determine the specific substances being abused as well as the quality and frequency of abuse'. They ask whether drug abuse precedes, follows or accompanies schizophrenia. However, they conclude that, 'The research evidence is equivocal in showing support for each of them' (ibid.). Similarly, Ries (1993) says that schizophrenics tend to use the substances that are most readily available, including alcohol, so that opportunity tends to determine use patterns. Other studies are more clear-cut in their findings, showing that schizophrenic patients will use more amphetamines, cocaine, cannabis and stimulant/hallucinogenics generally and less alcohol, opiates and sedative hypnotics than other substance misusers (Saloum et al. 1991). Other studies have shown the reverse, finding that alcohol is commonly used to self-medicate, especially to make the voices go away at times when the symptoms are worsening (Knudsen and Villmar 1984 quoted in ibid.). Castaneda et al. (1991) say that there is a clear link between schizophrenia and alcoholism – 22% of alcoholics were schizophrenics. 'Many alcoholics suffer an underlying schizophrenia' (ibid.). Cocaine use was also common.

Such agreement as exists about the types of drug taken is that few schizophrenics take heroin. This too is odd, because one would expect heroin to be used as a form of self-medication against the unpleasant symptoms of schizophrenia, or against its current treatment. A possible explanation is that the lifestyle and demands of life on the streets of an intravenous addict are too much for most schizophrenics. They would take the drugs if they could get them but:

> the constant need to obtain paraphernalia and heroin several times a day in order to prevent the onset of withdrawal symptoms could

exceed the resourcefulness of poorly functioning schizophrenics. (Castaneda et al. 1991, p. 318)

Clearly, heroin could be an effective form of self-medication.

Of equal interest is why schizophrenic patients take stimulants and hallucinogens. These drugs could be expected to enhance the strength of the hallucinations and aggravate rather than improve the disease condition. Cocaine use among schizophrenics produces a worsening of the primary psychiatric symptoms. Negrete et al. (op. cit.) noted an enhancement of hallucination among their sample population when they were using cannabis. It appeared to make the psychotic symptoms worse, or it produced a secondary toxic state superimposed on the first, or it heightened the effects of any anti-psychotic medication the patients were taking – the data were insufficient to differentiate between these three mechanisms. Castaneda et al. (1991) are more confident. They say that their data do not support the hypothesis that addiction is a complication of a primary psychiatric disorder, but that addiction in schizophrenics is similar to that of addiction in non-schizophrenics, that is, addiction in schizophrenics constitutes a separate disease entirely (p. 317). Castaneda et al. say that schizophrenic patients take drugs not to self-medicate, or for any other reason connected with their disorder; but that they take them for the same varied reasons as non-schizophrenics, and will continue to take them in spite of the effect on their disorders. There are, of course, other possibilities. Might it be that some schizophrenic patients take stimulants in order to add warmth and interest to their lives and to offset the coldness induced by their disorder? Schizophrenia is, after all, a lonely experience which cocaine, cannabis and LSD may help.

MICAs and CAMIs

In an attempt to pick a path through this minefield, I want to give examples of what I believe are comorbidities commonly seen in clinical practice. For convenience, and to draw out the various theoretical links, I have called them MICAs and CAMIs. Presented in this way, the assumption is that the links are real, not artefacts. This is not to ignore or bypass the sceptics, but is to help to refine some of the clinical variables which present themselves with dual diagnosis patients.

MICAs are defined as mental illness preceding substance abuse, where the two conditions are aetiologically linked (MICA is the acronym for Mental Illness Chemical Abuse). CAMIs are defined as chemical abuse preceding mental illness (CAMI is the acronym for Chemical Abuse Mental Illness, again where the two conditions are aetiologically linked). (Terms such as chemical abuse rather than substance abuse and mental illness rather than mental disorder have been used. This is to fit into common usage.)

Below are six examples of MICAs, by no means a complete list but large enough to be of interest.

1 The mentally ill person takes chemicals (illicit drugs) to ease his mental disorder, that is, to self-medicate. For example: a depressive patient may take stimulants such as amphetamines or crack/cocaine; a hypomanic patient may take depressants such as opiates, synthetic opiates or barbiturates to contain the mental disorder, or perhaps ease it in some way; and a schizophrenic patient may take opiates to dampen down the hallucinations, perhaps to improve his social functioning. The danger is that such self-medication will have the opposite effect and tip the patient further into mental disorder, or if not, then reduce the chances of treatment having any effect. The mental disorder is then masked by the self-medication, making it difficult, perhaps impossible, to make a diagnosis until the self-medication stops. The physician's only clue may be a past history of psychiatric disorder, which could alert him to the possibility that self-medication has occurred.

2 The mentally disordered person takes his form of chemical abuse to change the direction of the disorder, that is, not so much to self-medicate as to move the mental disorder to a different form. For example, a schizophrenic patient may take cannabis or ecstasy to produce different hallucinations, which are more durable and tolerable, or a depressive patient may take opiates to change the direction of the depression – again the latter condition may be more tolerable to the patient than the former.

3 The patient resorts to chemical abuse to overcome the effects of the prescribed psychiatric treatment, that is, the patient may dislike the effects of heavy tranquillisers and may take opiates to counteract these, or take stimulants to neutralise their effects.

4 The patient's lifestyle is centred on substance abuse, that is, where a strong cultural component exists and the patient finds that the way of life associated with chemical abuse is an agreeable one, producing a new status and a new image. It may also confer acceptance, as drug users may be less condemning about his behaviour. The attractions associated with the drug culture may allow the mentally disordered patient to fit into a world in which medicine and psychiatry

are discounted, or regarded as being providers of drugs rather than as capable of treating existing conditions.

5 The mental patient is exploited by, rather than integrated into, the drug culture. There is exploitation because drug users encourage the mentally disordered patient to take drugs and get him to pay for them at a higher rate.

6 The mental patient becomes disinhibited, that is, he may drink too much, take too many drugs and lose self-control. In this case, the mentally disordered patient is unable to make appropriate choices. He simply takes anything – drink or drugs – without regard to the consequences.

Then the CAMIs. I have listed five examples of CAMIs, again for the same reasons as with the MICAs.

1 Chemical abuse leads directly to mental illness. This is the most straightforward case and provides the most direct causal link. It exists where a psychosis develops, either as a result of the use of illicit drugs such as amphetamine, or even LSD (although some physicians dispute the existence of an LSD psychosis) or licit drugs such as alcohol.

2 Chemical abuse leads back to mental illness. Here the drug user may relapse into an older psychiatric condition, or perhaps have a more varied form of the existing disorder. For example, a schizophrenic patient in remission who takes amphetamines could easily relapse, or the direction of the schizophrenia may change as a result of the illicit drugs.

3 The use of drugs exacerbates an existing condition, producing more dramatic and florid symptoms than hitherto.

4 The drug user is a long-term user and is 'burned out'. Long-term amphetamine users often develop depression. Long-term heroin users also develop depression – the same problem applies as with the amphetamine use. It is almost as if the 'wiring' in their brain has been messed up by the long-term use of the drugs.

5 Finally, the withdrawal state itself leads to a mental disorder which can, in some circumstances, lead to chronicity. Treatment for this type of condition is usually ECT.

No data are available on the size of these groups, or how they interact with each other, or how each might differ in socio-demographic terms from the other. The British research evidence is simply not available, and American research is limited, although it suggests that patients with dual diagnosis are diagnosed differently and require more services than patients with a single diagnosis. They have higher rates of homelessness and extensive legal and medical problems, with more frequent and longer periods of hospitalisation and higher acute care utilisation rates (Ries 1994, p. 19). This makes it all the more important for clinicians to disaggregate the symptoms, or at least to be aware that the problem exists, so as to alert and refer to others.

The examples of MICAs and CAMIs provide only a brief checklist of this type of patient, based on anecdotal, clinical and observational methods. In many of the examples, a causal link can be inferred more strongly, in others we await more research.

Diagnosis

The problems of diagnosis are set out clearly in this quote below:

> Misdiagnosis of a psychotic episode induced by substance abuse is not uncommon, substance abuse is under diagnosed among psychotic patients and psychotic drug abuse usually receives a diagnosis of schizophrenia. (Saloum et al. 1991, p. 324)

The authors go on to say that some of the unfortunate consequences of these diagnostic uncertainties are to further complicate the clinical course and management of these patients (ibid.). The problems are that psychotic symptoms may be a result of:

(a)   substance abuse in a person otherwise not having a psychotic disorder
(b)   substance abuse by a person in which psychotic symptoms may have pre-existed the substance abuse
(c)   unrelated to substance abuse though persisting psychotic symptoms may be increased, altered, or even temporarily decreased as a result of the use of substances. (Ries 1993, p. 104)

Some clinicians make a primary/secondary distinction based on the sequence of the disorder, while others say that the sequence is either unavailable or unreliable, and, even if known, does not help in the immediate diagnosis, especially of an acute patient who is actively psychotic and currently a substance abuser (ibid. p. 104).

Whatever the procedure, the problems are the same: one condition can mimic, mask, precipitate and exacerbate the other, to the extent that substance abuse may be underdiagnosed among psychotic patients, or psychotic substance abusers receive another diagnosis, invariably schizophrenia, or mentally disordered patients are wrongly diagnosed or not diagnosed at all. For example, a stimulant-induced psychosis can resemble paranoid delusions, LSD effects can resemble schizophrenia and a phencyclidine psychosis can also resemble schizophrenia. One drug can mask or keep the mental disorder hidden, such as when alcohol is taken with schizophrenia, or cannabis taken with depression. That one condition can precipitate the other (usually a MICA) and exacerbate the other is emphasised by the following:

> Because they have two disorders they are vulnerable to drug relapse and a worsening of the psychiatric disorder... Addiction relapse often leads to psychiatric decompensation, and worsening of psychiatric problems often leads to addiction relapse. (Ries 1994, p. 4)

It was said in an earlier chapter that FMEs rarely provided an assessment of the offender's psychiatric condition, being more concerned with mental incapacity ('fit to be detained, fit to be interviewed'). Accordingly, many offenders with mental disorder were not diagnosed. How much more so with dual diagnosis? The American research shows the problems of diagnosing psychiatric conditions when they are mixed with drug abuse, not just diagnosis by physicians but by others working in the mental health or in the drug field. Ries put it this way:

> While most clinicians in the mental health system generally have an expertise... in the identification, diagnosis and treatment of psychiatric disorders, some lack similar skills and knowledge about the specific drugs of abuse, their processes of abuse and addiction... Similarly, treatment professionals may have a thorough understanding of drug abuse treatment but not of psychiatric treatment. (ibid. p. 10)

One solution is to introduce more screening programmes. Screening differs from diagnosis in that it is conducted early on in the process, typically preceding diagnosis, and is aimed at compiling information. The aim is to detect current mental health and substance abuse disorders, and identify those patients thought to be dual diagnosis patients (that is, those with the best predictors of dual diagnosis according to key variables such as age, gender and so on). Screening does not always require qualified physicians to be involved, trained non-medical personnel are adequate, as long as they are equipped with an appropriate, valid, screening instrument designed for effective identification. The aim is to pick up the cases for referral, where, at a later stage, a more certain diagnosis can be given. The American research is clear about the variables which act as the best predictors of dual diagnosis, and using these would make it easier to prepare a screening instrument to help to identify those cases. Screening does not have to be able to identify all patients with dual diagnosis, it is enough that it alerts doctors to the possibility of symptoms being present.

Screening is not a substitute for an effective diagnosis but it can help. Screening programmes could usefully be introduced where high levels of dual diagnosis patients are expected. Screening in police stations would be an important first step and help to ease the problems of diagnosis for FMEs. More certain diagnoses can be left until later, but that will always be a task for the specialists.

Treatment

Diagnosing patients is one thing, treating them is another. Two problems stand out: first, where should dual diagnosis patients be treated, and second, who should do the treatment? In the first, the problems are partly theoretical and partly about the extent of resources, and in the second, often revolve around the choices made by physicians who, more often than not, refuse to acknowledge that substance abuse is the problem or that substance abusers are their province (Bean 1998). There is an interesting debate going on in America concerning the priority and order in which the various conditions should be dealt with in the treatment of dual diagnosis patients. Three approaches have emerged, which we can call sequential, parallel and integrated (Bean 1998, p. 3).

The first approach is the sequential and supporters of this position argue that the patient should be treated first by one system and then the other – defined as the serial or non-simultaneous participation in both health and addiction settings (Ries 1994, p. 13). Those supporting the sequential programme believe that the dual conditions interact in such complex ways that is necessary to deal with one in order to understand the effect that it has on the second condition. The problem is to decide which to deal with first. Some clinicians argue that abstinence must come first before any assessment can be made of the psychiatric condition. Others argue for the psychiatric condition to be given priority, and still others argue that the most severe condition should be dealt with first. There are a small number who say that the most appropriate way to deal with the conditions is to take them in the order in which they occurred.

The second approach involves parallel treatment (ibid. p. 14). This is defined as the simultaneous involvement of the patient in both mental health and treatment settings. The argument here is that parallel treatment is preferred because to do otherwise is to leave one of the morbidities untreated, which would permit the untreated condition to exacerbate the treated condition. For example, untreated substance abuse will continue to aggravate any attempt to treat the psychiatric condition, because continuing use of illegal substances not only places the patient in a vulnerable condition vis-à-vis the law but the drugs themselves mask or mimic the psychiatric condition. Conversely an untreated psychiatric condition will make it difficult for the patient to meet the demands of substance abuse withdrawal, which is difficult enough at the best of times. But how to find clinicians of equal competence? Rarely in Britain are the drug treatment services as advanced as the psychiatric services, and only a few are run by medical personnel – this, incidentally, produces additional problems of confidentiality. It also increases the likelihood that the patient will receive conflicting treatment, where confrontational therapy might be the preferred option for drug treatment but considered inappropriate for psychiatric treatment, or where abstinence is the goal of drug treatment but not of the psychiatric services. (That problem is not confined to situations where treatment is provided by different agencies, but can and does exist within agencies.)

The third approach tries to meet these defects by integrating treatment into a unified programme. However, there are practical problems with an integrated programme, as few clinicians in Britain are sufficiently interested, let alone competent enough, to treat the two conditions. In one of the few British studies on dual diagnosis, Smith and Hucker (1994) suggest that treatment is best provided by the psychiatric services, and want them to be sufficiently flexible to prevent this highly vulnerable group being lost to psychiatry. But how to engage the interest of the psychiatrist when there are more rewarding and less disruptive patients to treat?

I said elsewhere (Bean 1998) that we should be less concerned with the ideal treatment programme and more with being able to recognise the problem, which means we need to sharpen our diagnostic skills and undertake some basic epidemiological research. I still retain that view, but am now concerned that we are not sufficiently interested in treatment to cope with an ever-increasing problem which shows no sign of going away, at least in the immediate future.

Links with legislation

At present Section 1(3) of the 1983 Act prohibits anyone being dealt with as mentally disordered 'by reason of promiscuity, or other immoral conduct, sexual deviancy or dependence on alcohol and drugs'. The Draft Outline Proposals of the Committee (Richardson 1999), considering changes to the 1983 Act, said:

> we do not wish to see this provision retained in its present form [because] the social context within which it was felt necessary has changed... With regard to substance misuse the prevailing view was that although substance abuse on its own should not be regarded as a mental disorder the prevalence of co-morbidity suggests that at the assessment stage at least it should not be excluded.

And in a key passage in its Draft Outline Proposal went on to say:

> The Committee would therefore recommend that the express exclusion be removed on the basis that in the absence of any underlying mental disorder substance abuse on its own could not meet the eventual criteria for compulsion. (Richardson 1999)

This passage is not at all clear. What I think it means is that the presence of substance abuse as a comorbid condition ought to be regarded in a different light than when it exists on its own. If that is so, and the government accepts this proposal, it will involve a distinct change in the government's strategy in dealing with mental disorder, and heralds a recognition of the way in which the disorders react and interact with each other.

However, the full Report of the Expert Committee (Department of Health 1999, paras 4.10 and 4.11) put a different view. It said that the responses to its earlier recommendations were mixed, and, although there was general agreement that comorbidity should be adequately treated, there was disagreement about how best to go about things. The Committee concluded that 'drug and alcohol misuse should be excluded as a *sole* (emphasis original) ground for believing mental disorder to be present' – that is, just because a patient is a substance misuser does not of itself indicate the presence of a mental disorder.

The Committee was 'very well aware of the relationship between substance abuse and violence' and recommended that any subsequent Code of Practice and relevant professional training emphasised the complex relationships between them.

What we are to be left with then, assuming Parliament accepts the Expert Committee Report, is a legislative framework which is no different than before, but an increasing problem of dual diagnosis. How best then to proceed? There is little doubt that some forms of substance abuse can mimic mental disorder, the use of amphetamines, for example, can produce signs and symptoms identical to that of paranoid schizophrenia, so much so that some psychiatrists object to the word 'mimic', as it appears to distort and degrade the condition. They say calling it a 'drug-induced psychosis' would be better. It remains perfectly legitimate to detain such a patient, assuming he fulfils the other necessary requirements for compulsory detention, and detention would be justified on the basis that an assessment is required before a full diagnosis is made. The aetiology is not important; mental disorder is mental disorder whatever the cause. Detention is possible whenever mental disorder occurs, be it as a drug-induced psychosis or otherwise.

So much for the legislative framework, what then of the practical realities? The problems of dual diagnosis will only be met if we are prepared to acknowledge that psychiatry has a key role in the treatment of substance abuse, and that substance misuse is seen as a psychiatric speciality, and not, as at present, a matter for drug treatment agencies. Advancing that cause will involve more than an increase in government funding, but a recognition that mainstream psychiatry must be more involved in matters which it has hitherto preferred to leave to others. Training programmes for psychiatrists need to be delivered urgently. It will not be easy to convince psychiatrists that they must treat these disruptive patients where, for all the reasons mentioned earlier, others, more deserving, yet due to a shortage of resources, remain untreated. But there is no other way. Dual diagnosis *is* a psychiatric problem, and will not go away, even if everyone, psychiatrists included, pretends that it does not exist.

Conclusion

I have wanted to show that the solution to the problem of dual diagnosis is not to be sought through legislation and the Expert Committee were correct in my view to leave things pretty much as before. The problem, however, is of such magnitude that it needs to be addressed quickly, as it will have a dramatic effect on psychiatric services in the near future. If the American data are anything to go by, we can, on a rough and ready basis, expect that about 50% of mentally disordered patients will be substance abusers, and that 50% of substance abusers will be mentally disordered. At present, the psychiatric services seem unprepared for that, and their response so far is to look in the other direction and presumably hope things will go away.

But that is not likely. If the integrity of mental health is to be preserved, then attention needs to be directed towards solutions, which, as I have suggested, will occur only as a result of more psychiatrists being involved with substance misuse services. That change is not likely to occur spontaneously; it will require more than a gentle push from government along with some financial inducement to health authorities to improve services. It is interesting that the Expert Committee invoked the question of public safety, urging that

> in terms of public safety we consider it essential that both the Code of Practice and the relevant professional training emphasise the complex relationship between substance misuse, mental disorder and violence. (1999, para. 4.11)

That would seem to be one of the clarion calls that may help move things along.

9

Psychiatric Services and Treatability

Whether a patient ends up in one control system or another is due often to contingencies. In effect, two control systems are in operation; a mental health system and a criminal justice system, one generally speaking taking non-offender patients, and the other taking offenders. I say generally speaking because things are rarely that straightforward. For example, the special hospitals take both types of patients, offenders and non-offenders alike, all detained in conditions of maximum security, and where non-offenders may remain detained longer. An offender may be charged with an offence and diverted out of the criminal justice system into the mental health system, the offence is then discounted, transforming the erstwhile offender into a civil patient. This is the so-called parallel system, where sometimes the systems work in harmony, sometimes not, and sometimes without an apparent regard for any other.

Insofar as there is a relevant official policy, the mental health (psychiatric) or non-offender system is given priority. The influential Home Office Circular 66/90 stated:

> It is government policy that wherever possible mentally disordered offenders should receive care and treatment from the health and social services. Where there is sufficient evidence... to show that a mentally disordered person has committed an offence careful consideration should be given to whether prosecution is required by the public interest. (Home Office 1990, para. 2)

What is particularly striking about this and similar statements is that rarely are challenges made to the assumptions on which they are based. The above quote implies that the criminal justice system is presumptively bad for the mentally disordered, while the health and social services are presumptively good. Certainly, many mentally disordered offenders receive little psychiatric treatment in the criminal justice system, and prisons are often unsuitable for such patients, but the prisoners themselves are not always critical of that. Of course, we ought not to base mental health policy on the views of individual prisoners, but mentally disordered offenders within the criminal justice system often cite two advantages that prison has over the health and social services. First, that the length of sentence is determined in advance – unless, of course, the offender is on a life sentence – and second, that mentally disordered offenders will not have to receive treatment while in prison. This, paradoxically, is seen as an advantage, as many will have received psychiatric treatment in the past, and their experiences may not always have been pleasant. There is, of course, nothing inherently virtuous about leaving patients untreated, but we should not assume automatically that, because a person has a psychiatric diagnosis, there will be benefits from treatment.

It is possible to detect something deeper in these comments, which relates to what Foucault called 'the battle for the offender's soul'. Foucault saw the criminal justice system and the psychiatric system as rival systems; lawyers and psychiatrists were, he said, in open competition. (He gave as an example the way psychiatrists offered a diagnostic term for each legal term: kleptomania for theft, infanticide for certain unlawful killings, pyromania for arson and so on. These are not very good examples and do not advance Foucault's case, so for the moment let us leave them aside and return to the main argument.) The mentally disordered provide the archetypal battleground: transferring patients out of the criminal justice system into the psychiatric services is a way of exemplifying that 'competition for souls'. More importantly, 'competitions for souls' becomes a thin disguise for 'competition for resources', which perhaps, after all, is what the competition is about.

'Competition for souls' shows itself in a number of ways. For example, the influential Reed Report (Department of Health 1992b) emphasises the value of training, calling for additional resources to back this up. But this request is not for more training generally, or for training to be extended to all who work in the two systems. It is a call for training to be given to those working in the criminal justice system – judges, probation officers and so on – by those working in mental health. Criminal justice personnel, it seems, 'need a better understanding of the needs of mentally disordered offenders' (Department of Health 1992b). Nowhere does Reed suggest that psychiatrists or mental health workers need to be trained by judges or probation officers in order that they may acquire 'a better understanding of the legal rights of patients'. Training, according to the Reed Report, is a one way street, and is, of course, an obvious conduit to promote psychiatric rather than legal values.

What alternatives are there? Some, it seems, are straightforward, involving minor changes, others are less so, and some involve thinking the unthinkable. One of the 'unthinkables' is to consider what I call the process of disaggregation, which means disentangling the criminal justice system from the health system, and encouraging each to go its separate way. Disaggregation does not mean that the two systems become entirely separate, for that is clearly impracticable. Rather, it means establishing the pre-eminence of one set of activities over that of another; for the criminal justice system that means establishing the pre-eminence of the offence, linked to an expectation of judicial control, where justice is more important than welfare. For the mental health system, it is about retaining the pre-eminence of psychiatric treatment without attempting to acquire patients from criminal justice. Some form of crossover, whether of patients or staff, is likely to remain; for example, no one doubts that the NHS should be responsible for the treatment of all patients in the community and perhaps even in the prisons, but that does not mean offenders, whether they are prisoners or not, have to be transferred or diverted out of the criminal justice system. What is suggested here is the promotion of a stronger identity in each system, with the emphasis on promoting differences. In practice, that means placing more emphasis on the criminal justice system to treat its mentally disordered, and to develop its own treatment programmes, with the main allegiance to criminal justice values. That will not be easy, although Grendon Underwood prison has managed it successfully and provides a model for the future.

Disaggregation is not a new idea. Many years ago no less an authority than Norval Morris said that where health and criminal justice systems merge both lose; the health system loses because non-offenders are excessively controlled, and the criminal justice system because offenders are detained under indeterminate conditions. Notions of justice are lost (Morris 1980). Other critics have challenged the role of the special hospitals and the manner in which they mix offenders and non-offenders alike, while others have questioned the wisdom of some diversion schemes. Disaggregation is, however, unlikely to be accepted as government policy, at least in the near future; the Reed Report is more fashionable and more in tune with government thinking. It is not beyond the realms of possibility that its day may come, although any move to disaggregation will not be straightforward. At present these criticisms are no more than straws in the wind, but may one day be regarded as more acceptable.

One such straw was the publication in 1999 of a damning report on Ashworth Special Hospital (Department of Health 1999b), which highlighted that perennial question: should the mad and the bad be mixed together? Within the context of that inquiry: is Ashworth a hospital or a prison? In one sense Ashworth is a hospital; the Department of Health runs it and its patients are treated according to the requirements of medicine (psychiatry). But it is also a prison: it is a high security institution where patients can neither determine their treatment nor choose when to leave. (That it was, according to *The Times* (6 August 1997), run unofficially by the Prison Officers Association, backed by the connivance of weak management, merely adds to its predicament: it does not affect the basic question about its role as a secure institution for offenders and non-offenders alike.) Support too can be found in the Fallon Report on Ashworth Hospital which opted for a form of disaggregation for patients diagnosed as having personality disorders. It said:

> We can find no rational justification for keeping this very manipulative and troublesome group [with personality disorder] in expensive therapeutic units providing management and treatment techniques for which they gain no benefit. (Department of Health 1999b)

Special hospitals provide but one example of the way in which the offender and non-offender are mixed; there are others, although not on the same scale as the special hospitals. They raise the same question: are we to treat or punish? Are we to make the offender better or stop the criminality? Or are we to do both? In Britain we seem not to prefer to operate the parallel system of justice, which more accurately should be called a merged system.

Is it not time we began to rethink our strategy? That is, to take stock of our current position and see how things might improve. In the light of the aim of this book, as stated in Chapter 1, which is to protect public safety yet retain the integrity of mental health, might that rethink begin with a challenge to some of our basic assumptions, one of which is contained in Home Office Circular 66/90. This Circular made it government policy that 'wherever possible mentally disordered offenders should receive care and treatment from the health and social services' (Home Office 1990). I suggest this Circular has directed policy towards the merged system, and in so doing helps to muddle the aims. It has also blurred the essential differences between the patients, that is, one group are offenders (mad and bad) and the other are not (mad). It has also provided the platform for much anti-criminal justice thinking producing unnecessary tensions between the psychiatric services and criminal justice. I realise that posing the question in this way implies that offenders who are mad should remain in the criminal justice system when popular demand is otherwise, but I suggest that some of the answers to the questions posed throughout this book are to separate the two systems. That means the bad who are also mad stay in the criminal justice system, and the mad who are not bad stay in the psychiatric system.

Were the systems to be seperated, it would involve changes in thinking and practice. Placing offender populations under the control of criminal justice and non-offender populations under the control of the psychiatric services would establish clearer lines of authority and accountability. There can be no better example where these were not established than with the so-called psychiatric Probation Order where the Probation Order is run by the probation service (criminal justice) and treatment is provided by the psychiatrist (psychiatric services). As a result, it is rarely clear where the lines of accountability lie, so that no one, including the offender, knows what is expected. (In this respect it is interesting that, under the new Treatment and Testing Order for drug offenders, the psychiatrist providing the treatment will be directly accountable to the probation officer.)

Changes of the type suggested here would be slow. Home Office Circular 66/90 articulated many of the wishes of those who see the criminal justice system in less than favourable terms. Even the terminology used in everyday life supports the aims of the Circular. We talk of the 'mentally disordered offender' rather than the 'offender who is mentally disordered'. That is, we emphasise the mental disorder rather than the offence and in doing so follow the conclusion of the Reed Report (Department of Health 1992b), which assumed that the primary aim is to identify and treat the mental disorder, the offence being of secondary importance. When we talk of the offender who is mentally disordered, the emphasis shifts to retaining the primary aim, which is to protect the public interest, yet secures the right of the victims and provides the offender with the legal protection commensurate with his status.

Circular 66/90 has been able to attach a strong humanitarian (moral) overtone to the debate which will be difficult to pass over. The Reed Committee also saw the need to provide treatment for all the mentally disordered, offender and non-offender alike. Criminal justice was seen as presumptively bad for the mentally disordered, while the psychiatric system was presumptively good. Nowhere did the Reed Committee suggest that treatment could be provided in criminal justice, or that there were dangers with psychiatric treatment anyway, or acknowledge an alternative. They wanted treatment to be given, and as speedily as possible. One way to challenge the Reed Committee and question their assertion that there is a straightforward humanitarian link underlying their position is to challenge some of the basic assumptions on which it rests. The first is to question their assertion that psychiatric treatment is always benevolent, with delays in treatment reprehensible. Yet:

> For every patient you can show me whose treatment is delayed...
> I can show you [those] who were improperly medicated in the past
> and suffered needless side effects as a result. (quoted in Applebaum
> 1994, p. 127)

The Reed Committee imply that avoiding justice through the provision of psychiatric services is an acceptable moral position. Again, we need to question this. They do not see that it may complicate matters, for in escaping justice, these patients may be putting themselves in greater jeopardy. Jill Peay makes the point in a slightly different form, when she wonders if positive discrimination, that is, being given treatment and therefore avoiding a sentence of the court, does not turn out to be negative discrimination after all.

> For a normal offender not on a life sentence imprisonment means
> the prospect of a certain release combined with the possibility of
> parole, while a patient on a restriction order has the prospect of pro-
> longed indefinite detention combined with the ongoing possibility of
> release occurring earlier in the period of confinement. Does treat-
> ment make this a price worth paying? Is it one that can be justified?
> Has what has been held out in theory as positive discrimination been
> negative discrimination in practice? (Peay 1993, p. 51)

Others point out how psychiatric provisions have become a variable commodity. Sometimes treatment promotes positive discrimination, where the allurement of treatment is held as an encouragement to play down the importance of the offence, as with diversion. Sometimes it provides negative discrimination, as in the special hospitals, where the possibility exists of the offender remaining in custody for longer than had he been sentenced for the offence. I do not want to get into a position where psychiatric treatment is seen negatively, but I do want to show that it cannot always be presumed to be good.

The standard objection to the proposal that the systems be separated is that the patients, offender and non-offender alike, are but one and the same. For example, it would be suggested that those patients detained on a Section 136 are likely to have a lengthy criminal record, or that dual diagnosis patients will be offenders – how else did they acquire their habit? So, it is said, to talk of offender and non-offender patients as if they were separate groups or to suggest that Section 136 or dual diagnosis patients were non-offenders is to distort reality.

There is overlap, but there are also differences. The socio-demographic composition of detained mental hospital non-offender patients does not match those mentally disordered offenders in prison, nor is their criminal history similar. Nor is it acceptable to suggest that, because a group of patients were once offenders, and still may be for all we know, they should be dealt with on the presumption that they still are. They, like the rest of us, are entitled to a presumption of innocence. I am aware that patients with a history of convictions are likely to be disruptive on the wards and demanding of services, but that is a management problem, and should not be the basis on which a policy is promoted.

What direction can we take? If we shift the emphasis to the offender who is mentally disordered, does this make things easier? In one sense, yes, for it gives the responsibility to the criminal justice system and accountability and authority are established through that. It will still be a slow process, but we can begin by identifying areas needing immediate attention and work from there.

Treatability

The demands of community safety have been ever present. These will not easily go away nor should they, for the questions they pose require answers. The difficulty is that some of the answers may not turn out to be of our liking, or will appear as a mixed blessing – the most controversial coming from the Home Secretary, which we can call the treatability test. This is worth considering at some length, for the implications are startling, affecting the care of patients in the community as well as elsewhere.

What we call the treatability test, the Home Secretary calls 'an impediment to public safety' (*The Times*, 13 February 1999). 'Treatability' has a long, winding history. It begins with the Percy Commission Report (1957) and it ends, for the moment, with the Home Secretary announcing a new indeterminate sentence. This is to be imposed on criminals convicted of violent and sexual offences, who are not considered treatable under the current mental health laws (*The Times*, 13 February 1999). Mr Straw told MPs:

There is a group of dangerous and severely personally disordered individuals from whom the public are not properly protected and who are neither restrained effectively by the criminal law nor mental health provisions. Their propensity to commit the most serious sexual and violent acts may be well known and recorded. (ibid.)

A consultation paper followed, setting out where such offenders could be detained, that is, either in prisons or special hospitals, or in a completely new network of secure units – as suggested earlier by the Fallon Report (Department of Health 1999b, see Recommendation 47, p. 402). Noting that these proposals were 'a serious step', the Home Secretary promised safeguards, including regular quasi-judicial reviews of the sentences (*The Times*, 16 February 1999).

On the face of it, the debate is about a group of psychopathic offenders who are dangerous and need control. But it goes deeper: it extends beyond the proposals for a new sentence. It involves decisions by psychiatrists who are reluctant to admit patients to their hospitals who they consider 'not treatable', but where the courts and others suspect that 'not treatable' is a euphemism for 'not wanting to treat'. (A typical example would be when a court wants to make a Hospital Order but no hospital will accept the patient, or where patients in special hospitals cannot be discharged because no one will take them. They remain in conditions of greater security than is otherwise necessary.) It spreads into and around the Fallon Report, which talks of the 'dreadful confusion between the function of the prison and Special Hospital for psychopathic offenders' (op. cit.).

Before looking at 'treatability' in its legal sense, consider first the civil rights questions surrounding the Home Secretary's proposal. He wants to provide protection from those 'severely personally disordered individuals' who 'have a propensity to commit the most serious sexual and violent acts'. That is to say, he wants the courts to be given powers to order the indefinite detention of such individuals, whether or not they had committed an offence. Detention would be reviewed and the offender released, only when he no longer posed a 'grave risk to the public'. *The Times* describes the problem this way:

At present individuals with non-treatable personality disorders slip though the net between hospital – where they can only be detained if they are diagnosed as 'treatable' – and prison, where they can only remain for the duration of their sentence. High profile cases have added urgency to Mr Straw's call to close this loophole. (22 February 1999)

Opposition to this proposal comes mainly from civil rights organisations and some members of the legal profession, who see it as a violation of common law rights. One lawyer quoted Magna Carta, 'No free man shall be taken or imprisoned save by lawful judgement of his peers', suggesting this be compulsory reading for the Home Secretary (*The Times*, 22 February 1999). Another, an ex-High Court Judge, points out that the wicked, that is, offenders with a moral sense, will, under the Home Secretary's proposal, be let off rather more lightly than those without a moral sense, that is, those with the untreatable personality disorder will be detained but those who are just plain wicked will not. Others argue that this proposal allows individuals to be detained, not for what they have done, but for what they might do. For example, a spokesman for the Bar Council is reported as saying 'Plans to lock someone up before they have committed a crime need to be examined extremely carefully given the presumption of innocence in our legal system' (*The Times*, 16 February 1999).

It is said that the Home Secretary has been forced to react, because of growing public alarm at the release from prison of a small number of dangerous paedophiles, and because of public anger over high-profile cases where psychiatrists have not considered the patient's condition treatable; the offender being sent to prison rather than hospital. These high-profile cases, media led and highly selective, produce correspondingly high levels of fear of crime, and high levels of fear of crime produce demands to sacrifice civil rights, which are seen to favour the offender rather than the victim. However, set against the rights of the offender must be the rights of the public who need protection against these violent criminals. We are left with the obvious dilemma; whose rights are more important? Stated in this stark form, most would say the victim, for the life of the victim becomes more important than the legal rights of the offender, who at worst faces a period of imprisonment.

A distinction can be made between an indeterminate sentence subject to review – this being for those convicted of an offence – and a sentence imposed before the crime has been committed. The crucial difference is that in one case an offender is detained having been lawfully convicted for an offence, and the other is detained on the basis of a predicted offence. Britain has never had an indeterminate sentence whereby an offender is detained until ready to be discharged – except the life sentence for very specific crimes such as murder – although there have been semi-indeterminate sentences where the offender is released within a maximum and minimum period. Had the Home Secretary confined himself to these semi-indeterminate sentences made after an offence was committed, it is likely that the opposition would have been more muted; there is, after all, a difference between deciding when to let someone out, having committed an offence, and deciding when to lock someone up who has not committed an offence. (There are of course, certain similarities: the criteria to continue detention is often couched in vague terms, and there remains the puzzling question as to who is competent enough to make the decision.)

The demands for public safety are now so strong that we have become accustomed to legislation which would have been unthinkable a generation ago. Consider the reviewable sentence, where an organisation such as the National Association for the Care and Resettlement of Offenders (NACRO), traditionally on the side of the civil rights of offenders, backs proposals for a reviewable sentence for dangerous offenders with severe personality disorders. That NACRO wants these offenders housed outside the prison and hospital systems hardly mollifies the obvious objections. We have the Sex Offenders Act requiring selected sex offenders to register with the police; and we have Public Protection Panels – who consider these sex offenders and other offenders brought to its notice who its members consider dangerous – staffed by representatives of the police, the probation service and the local authority. All move us in that same direction.

How many such offenders is the Home Secretary expecting to include in his proposal, and how many deaths or serious injuries is he expecting to save? How many false positives is he prepared to accept? Is there an acceptable rate of false positives and if so what is it? Has he considered an inevitable consequence of his proposal, which is that a special purpose-built unit with 5 beds will be filled, as it will if it had 50, 100, or 500 beds? Filling beds provides no guidelines to the number of potentially dangerous offenders in the community; all the evidence suggests that the take-up rate is always such as to fill the available space. And what effect will the Home Secretary's proposal have on the subsequent diagnosis of mental disorder? The Director of the Schizophrenia Association regards the proposed legislation as 'spine chilling' and says it must be resisted:

> If it were enacted severely mentally ill people suffering from schizophrenia and their families would not be free of the fear that it would be the easiest thing in the world for a psychiatrist to change their diagnosis to psychopathy so that they could be locked up for an indeterminate time having committed no criminal act. (*The Times*, 22 February 1999)

There is a sense of déjà vu about much of this. One is reminded of the debates surrounding the proposals for a Community Treatment Order, where little evidence was produced to justify its introduction but much was made about the fear of crime and public protection. The civil libertarians lost that debate, and this one may be lost as well. Public protection is a powerful force, capable of driving the argument to the point where traditional freedoms can be put aside.

Personality disorder or psychopathy – the terms can be used interchangeably – are not the only psychiatric conditions that are untreatable. Presumably the difference is that these conditions are more common in the criminal classes but leave that aside for the moment. The debate has raised other questions which are about the role of psychiatry within society; has psychiatry a duty to care for patients even if the patients' condition is untreatable? Dementia, or Alzheimer's disease, is not treatable but should psychiatry walk away from patients with that condition? Mentally impaired children are not treatable but are they to be discarded too? If not, what distinguishes the patient with an untreatable personality disorder from those with dementia or mental impairement? Should psychiatry be given the choice of walking away from these? Can psychiatry, especially that which operates within the NHS and is a branch of the state, walk away from a group of patients because it chooses to do so? (Objections may be made about 'psychiatry as an arm of the state', on the grounds that, as part of the profession of medicine, its members are an independent professional group, but it is the state that employs them, whether in special or public hospitals, and no amount of claims to professional independence will change that.)

An obvious solution would be for the state to tell psychiatrists to treat patients with personality disorders and see that they get on with it. Psychiatrists, like other state employees, should be expected to do what they are told. The state could do this of course, but it may not work; professions have the collective power to disrupt government and it is likely they would do so here. An alternative would be to try to persuade the medical profession that people suffering from serious personality disorders could be treated, a move no doubt considered by the Home Secretary but put aside as presumably he thought it would take too long. Hence his proposal which is aimed at avoiding a confrontation or a lengthy debate, but which, incidentally, may not turn out to be successful.

To complicate matters further, the psychiatric position is at one level entirely defensible. There is, psychiatrists would say, no justification for taking patients into treatment and using up scarce resources on those who are not, in their professional opinion, treatable. There is little point in using up a bed for a patient who will not respond to treatment, when in doing so others more capable of being treated could be provided with those facilities. And this, at a time when resources are stretched – there is a national shortage of psychiatrists in Britain – and where hospital beds are at a premium. Moreover, personality disordered patients are long stay and chronic. They are also disruptive, reduce staff morale, and take up a disproportionate amount of staff time. Whenever there are patients with a personality disorder in a ward, deterioration occurs in the ward atmosphere, especially in matters of ward discipline, with high levels of non-compliance.

How best then to proceed? We need to go back to the origin of the term and see where that leads us. 'Treatability' is not a legal term, that is, there is no legal definition of treatability within the legislation. Under Sections 2 and 3 of the 1983 Act, patients who are not treatable in hospital cannot be detained, and, of course, if not detained, then cannot be given treatment against their will. It has entered modern mental health legislation in a way hardly intended by the Percy Commission (1957), and in a way which 'is designed to protect the hospitals from any responsibility towards patients whom they do not want, but it provides no protection at all for the patient who does not want the hospital' (Gunn 1979).

Brenda Hoggett (1984, pp. 60–2) has described the history of treatability within the existing legislation. The Percy Commission proposed it first for the protection of all patients, but the 1983 Act restricted it to the psychopathic and the non-severely mentally impaired. As regards the psychopath, the Percy Commission wanted to protect this group of patients from being detained before their antisocial (criminal) tendencies were made known. (It did not want to produce the same problems as with young unmarried mothers under earlier legislation, who had not been protected and had been confined as 'moral defectives'.) Where there were similarities, that is, the patient was under the age of 21 and had shown criminal tendencies, the Commission thought they could be detained for a short period of observation to improve their behaviour while growing up. Once passed the age of 21 – although if they had been admitted before that age, they could be kept until 25 – they should not be compelled to enter hospital (ibid. p. 60).

Brenda Hoggett says that in the years that followed that point was forgotten, and the age limit was seen as an arbitrary restriction upon the hospitals' powers to provide treatment when they thought it might do good. That it might not in many cases – psychopaths do not readily respond to treatment – was not the point. It may do so occasionally and there was no reason to exclude those, if they were over the age of 21.

Hence the age limit was swept away. And so, under the 1983 Act, for an admission for treatment for psychopathy (and for mental impairment), it must be such that hospital treatment 'is likely to alleviate or prevent a deterioration of the patient's condition' (ibid. p. 60). If it is not, then admission is not justified.

The treatability condition, which is what it has now become, has provided psychiatrists with the right to declare patients 'not treatable' and for the hospitals to say 'not suitable for admission'. It gives hospitals the right to avoid admitting such patients – 'many hospitals have been reluctant to accept these patients for years' says Brenda Hoggett (p. 61). And it is this that the Home Secretary sees as unacceptable. He wants power to detain those who may not be treatable, and who may also be potentially criminal, especially the violent. Operating from the position of protecting public safety, the Home Secretary wants to direct attention at that group of patients, who may not be convicted offenders, but who are nonetheless likely to commit offences.

> There is a group of dangerous and severely personally disordered individuals from whom the public are not properly protected and who are neither restrained effectively by the criminal law nor mental health provisions. Their propensity to commit the most serious sexual and violent acts may be well known and recorded. (*The Times*, 16 February 1999)

Is there a way around existing legislation? For example, 'medical treatment' under the 1983 Act (Section 145) includes 'nursing and care and rehabilitation under medical supervision'. Why not bypass the psychiatrists and allow treatment to take place under the supervision of a social worker or nursing officer? The difficulty with this is that psychiatrists run the treatment team and are the Responsible Medical Officers, that is, responsible for *all* treatments. Bypassing the psychiatrists is not, then, an option.

Why not then simply remove psychopathy (and its later variation 'personality disorder') from the legislation altogether? That would have the obvious effect of pleasing numerous psychiatrists: 'We can see no natural justification for keeping this very manipulative and troublesome sub group in expensive therapeutic units providing management and treatment techniques for which they gain no benefit' (Department of Health 1999b, para. 6.10.11) but it would not meet the Home Secretary's wishes. He wants this group of patients detained before they commit further offences: he wants to use the Mental Health Acts as a way of enforcing preventative detention. Taking this category of patients out of the legislation would not, for the Home Secretary, do at all, for it would not meet his basic requirement. He might agree with Estella Baker and John Crighton (1995, p. 118) that the treatability test 'has preserved the rights of doctors to protect themselves from psychopathically disordered patients whom they do not wish to treat at the expense of the rights of the patients themselves', but he wants doctors to agree to detain and treat this group of patients. The problem will not go away by slow reform involving amending categories, a point made by Coid, who says 'proposals to abandon the legal category psychopathic disorder are irrelevant and merely serve to obscure more important issues' (quoted in ibid. p. 118).

The solution for the Home Secretary may be to change the legal categories, including removing from the Mental Health Act all references to psychopathy and personality disorder and its corresponding treatability test (leaving treatability for the mentally impaired would make little difference and not affect matters). New legislation would allow psychopathic patients convicted of an offence to be detained in prison and be given treatment in special units along the lines of Grendon Underwood prison. This would remove offenders from the so-called lottery, a term used in the Fallon Report, when it said, 'whether or not a convicted offender is diagnosed as suffering from psychopathic disorder and becomes the subject of a hospital order is to a considerable extent a matter of chance' (Department of Health 1999b, para. 6.3.1), but it would still leave unresolved that aspect involving preventative detention, with all the threats to civil liberties that entails.

Underlying the Home Secretary's proposals is something deeper. Treatability is the thin end of a much larger wedge about medical discretion within the criminal justice/special hospital system, whereby psychiatrists are permitted to decide whom to accept in their hospitals. Under Section 37 of the 1983 Mental Health Act, before making a Hospital Order, with or without restriction, a judge must consider any recommendations made by two doctors, one of whom must be approved for these purposes under Section 12(2) of the 1983 Act. Medical recommendations must specify the class of mental disorder present, the doctors must agree, and a bed must be available in an appropriate hospital. If not, the order cannot be made and the offender will likely go to prison, even if mentally ill. Often courts have wanted to make an order but have been frustrated because no bed could be found, or no hospital would agree to accept the patient.

The 'lottery' which exists for psychopaths exists also for those suffering from other categories of mental disorder. In a paper to the Fallon Committee, Dr Chiswick asked, 'Do the 400 psychopaths detained in

Special Hospitals share common clinical features that are absent in the thousands of violent men who are processed through the penal system' (Department of Health 1999b, para. 6.3.6). Substitute 'mentally ill' for 'psychopath', 'mental hospital' for 'Special Hospital', delete '400' and 'violent', and then ask, 'Do the unknown number of mentally ill detained in hospital share common clinical features that are absent in the thousands of men who are processed through the penal system' and the question becomes equally relevant. Who finishes up where, for how long and for whatever reason remains one of the great unanswered questions.

The law is a blunt instrument when it comes to requiring psychiatrists to take patients they are otherwise unwilling to take. Judges rarely involve themselves in clinical decisions, preferring to concentrate on procedures. Decisions, they would say, are for the professionals. That is why treatability is important: it opens up questions of psychiatric discretion, where psychiatrists rightly say there is no point in directing resources at patients they regard as untreatable, and the government sees 'unable to treat' as a euphemism for 'not wanting to treat'.

There is also that question of the role of psychiatry within the criminal justice system. The two features in this chapter, that relating to the prison medical service and to treatability, are but two from a host of questions which remain unasked and unanswered. The Fallon Report summed up the problem:

> Detaining custodial institutions have two aims, one therapeutic the other custodial. These... should be complimentary but there is a tendency for these functions to polarise out and eventually split like living cells into two separate institutions. (Department of Health 1999b, para. 7.12.14)

As indeed there is, to the detriment of all concerned.

Conclusion

To return to the main theme of this book; I have regarded community safety with some suspicion, not because the questions being asked by the community safety lobby are wrong, or irrelevant. Quite the reverse. But within community safety there are strands or extremes which I regard with deep suspicion, for they are committed to increasing the levels of controls, threatening certain civil rights, and moving us in the direction where the mentally disordered are seen as an unreasonable

threat to public welfare. In my view, it is only through a careful examination of our institutions that the threat can be met and overcome.

In the first section of this book, I wanted to seek justifications about
compulsory powers. Without that, it seems we are in danger of losing
our anchorage and our bearings. If the assumption is made that
compulsion is self-evidently acceptable, requiring no justification
except perhaps concerning the logistics of conveying patients to the
appropriate institutions, then there is no telling where things will go.
We could find ourselves accepting all sorts of proposals which could
involve compelling patients to receive treatment under all sorts of
conditions, and in all sorts of settings – some on the basis that patients
will be grateful for the intervention. The 'thank you theory' of psychiatry is most persuasive, yet potentially dangerous to the civil rights of
the patients.

In this first section I also wanted to show that the type of justification
for compulsion presented in the Expert Committee's Report (Department of Health 1999) is inadequate and, by implication, a cause of
much concern; the Committee justified compulsion on the grounds that
'where a patient lacks the capacity to consent to care and treatment
for mental disorder, then society should have the power to provide
that care and treatment even in the absence of that person's consent'
(para. 4.1). As we do not compel those lacking capacity to do many
other things, why should they be compelled to receive treatment for
mental disorder? Quite simply, that justification provided by the Committee and in that form will not do. It offers carte blanche to do anything
to anyone lacking capacity, and for that reason is worrying, and it arises
because there was no attempt – as illustrated in the Report – to look
further at what justifications are acceptable.

I have also tried to show that community supervision in Britain, in its
current form, requires a more careful examination. In the reductionist
approach to controls that I have adopted here, it is difficult to justify
the introduction and continued use of Supervision Registers, and no
less comfortable to see the ease with which the Expert Committee slips
into making its proposals for a Compulsory Treatment Order in the
community. There is little or no discussion about its effects, and nothing
about its justification. This illustrates the point made above; that we
have tacitly accepted controls which a decade or so earlier would have
been unthinkable, and with little or no evidence as to their effectiveness. One wonders how far we shall continue on that road before deciding
enough is enough.

I have also tried to show how other features need to be kept in repair,
and sometimes greatly improved to bring them up to standard. The

Appropriate Adult scheme is poorly developed, and needs to be given a greater measure of priority than at present. The role and function of the FME needs to be re-examined, if only to help to meet the increasing pressures placed on the police to deal with the mentally disordered, whether as civil patients or as offenders. I have also wanted to look closely at diversion, believing this to be another area where a sceptical approach would pay dividends. Diversion is, after all, one of those activities with which almost everyone seems to be in favour, yet few seem to see that it has implications which are less than benign. Dual diagnosis points to the future, showing where and how we must direct some of our resources.

Adopting a reductionist perspective helps, I think, to avoid some of the more obvious traps that beset any traveller in this area. It is all too easy to see a problem and, in one's eagerness to find a solution, to believe that more controls are the answer, or indeed that a solution exists. A lesson from the 1960's labelling theorists is one that needs to be relearned: that the solution becomes part of the problem. If the problem that is being created is not to be too large, then tread cautiously, and assume that there are always minefields present which will make everything worse. We have a propensity for making things worse, and, when it comes to dealing with the mentally disordered, that propensity and their vulnerability is greater than most.

References

Appelbaum P. (1994) *Almost a Revolution*. Oxford University Press.

Audit Commission (1998) *The Doctors Bill. The Provision of Forensic Medical Services to the Police*. Audit Commission.

Baker E. (1997) The Introduction of Supervision Registers in England and Wales: A Risk Communications Analysis. *Journal of Forensic Psychiatry*. **8**(1): 15–35.

Baker E. and Crighton J. (1995) *Ex parte A*: Psychopathy, Treatability and the Law. *Journal of Forensic Psychiatry*. **6**(1): 101–19.

Baldwin J. (1982) The Role of Interrogation in Crime Discovery and Conviction. *British Journal of Criminology*. **22**(2): 165–75.

Bean P.T. (1980) *Compulsory Admissions to Mental Hospitals*. John Wiley.

Bean P.T. (1986) *Mental Disorder and Legal Control*. Cambridge University Press.

Bean P.T. (1996) America's Drug Courts. A New Development in Criminal Justice. *Criminal Law Review*. (October) pp. 718–21.

Bean P.T. (1998) Dual Diagnosis and Beyond. *Alcohol Update*. (37): 2–3.

Bean P.T. (1999) The Police and the Mentally Disordered in the Community. In Webb D. and Harris R. (eds) *Mentally Disordered Offenders*. Routledge. pp. 38–52.

Bean P.T. and Mounser P. (1993) *Discharged from Mental Hospitals*. Macmillan.

Bean P.T. and Mounser P. (1994) The Community Treatment Order: Proposals and Prospects. *Journal of Social Policy*. **23**(1): 71–80.

Bean P.T. and Nemitz T. (1993) *Out of Depth and Out of Sight*. Report to MENCAP.

Bean P.T. and Nemitz T. (1994) The Use of the Appropriate Adult Scheme. A Preliminary Report. *Medicine, Science and the Law*. **34**(2): 161–6.

Bean P.T. and Nemitz T. (1997) The Treatment of Drug Misusers in Police Custody. *Journal of Substance Abuse*. **2**(1): 36–41.

Bell D.S. (1965) Comparisons of Amphetamine Psychosis and Schizophrenia. *British Journal of Psychiatry*. **111**: 701–7.

Bingley W. (1985) Mental Health Legislation in England and Wales. In Jensen K. and Pedersen B. *Commitment and Civil Rights of the Mentally Ill*. Sind Publishers. pp. 197–203.

Blom-Cooper L., Grounds A., Guiman P., Parker A. and Taylor M. (1996) *The Case of Jason Mitchell: Report of the Independent Panel of Enquiry*. Gerald Duckworth.

Bluglass R. (1983) *A Guide to the Mental Health Act 1983*. Churchill Livingstone.

Blumenthal S. and Wessely S. (1992) National Survey of Current Arrangements for Diversion from Custody in England and Wales. *British Medical Journal*. **305**: 1322–5.

British Association of Social Workers (1977) *Mental Health Crisis Services. A New Philosophy*. BASW.

Brown V., Ridgely M.S. and Pepper B. (1989) The Dual Crisis: Mental Illness and Substance Abuse. *American Psychologist*. (March) pp. 565–9.

Bynoe I. (1993) The Role of Criminal Justice Agencies: the Diversion of Mentally Disordered Offenders. In Mental Health Foundation, *Diversion Care and Justice* (Pre Conference Briefing Pack) pp. 25–33.

Caldicott F. (1994) Supervision Registers: The College's Response. *Psychiatric Bulletin*. **18**: 385–6.

Castaneda R., Galanter M., Lifshutz H. and Franco H. (1991) Effects of Drugs of Abuse on Psychiatric Symptoms among Hospitalised Schizophrenics. *American Journal of Drug Alcohol Abuse*. **17**(3): 313–20.

Cavadino P. (1999) Diverting Mentally Disordered Offenders from Custody. In Webb D. and Harris R. (eds) *Mentally Disordered Offenders*. Routledge. pp. 53–71.

Charlewood P. and Fender A. (1993) Purchasing Services for Mentally Disordered Offenders. In Mental Health Foundation, *Diversion Care and Justice*. pp. 14–18.

Cohen S. (1985) *Visions of Social Control*. Polity Press.

Cooke D.J. (1991) Treatment as an Alternative to Prosecution: Offenders Diverted for Treatment. *British Journal of Psychiatry*. **158** (June): 785–91.

Department of Health (1983) *Code of Practice on the Implementation of the Mental Health Act 1983*. HMSO.

Department of Health (1990) *The Care Programme Approach for People with a Mental Illness Referred to the Specialist Psychiatric Services*. HC(90)23, LASSL(90)11.

Department of Health (1992a) *Health of the Nation*. Cm. 1523. HMSO.

Department of Health (1992b) *Review of Health and Social Services for Mentally Disordered Offenders and Others Requiring Similar Services*. Final Summary Report (The Reed Report). Cm. 2088. HMSO.

Department of Health (1994) *Introduction of Supervision Registers for Mentally Ill People from 1 April 1994*. (*Health Service Guidelines*) HSG(94)5.

Department of Health press release (1998a) The Third Way for Mental Health.

Department of Health press release (1998b) Paul Boateng's Speech to the External Reference Group. Safe, Sound and Supportive Mental Health Services for the New Millenium.

Department of Health (1999) Report of the Expert Committee. *Review of the Mental Health Act 1983*.

Department of Health (1999a) Report by the Joint Prison Service and National Health Service Executive Working Group. *The Future Organisation of Prison Health Care*.

Department of Health (1999b) Report of the Committee of Inquiry into the Personality Disorder Unit at Ashworth Special Hospital. Vol. 1. (The Fallon Report) Cm. 4194-11. The Stationery Office.

Department of Health/Home Office (1978) *Review of the Mental Health Act 1959*. Cmnd. 7320. HMSO.

Department of Health/Home Office (1991) *Review of Health and Social Services for Mentally Disordered Offenders and Others Requiring Similar Services*. Report of the Prison Advisory Group.

Eastman N. (1997) The Mental Health (Patients in the Community) Act 1995. A Clinical Analysis. *British Journal of Psychiatry*. **170** (June): 492–6.

Eastman N. and Peay J. (1999) Law without Enforcement. Theory and Practice. In Eastman N. and Peay J. (eds) *Law without Enforcement*. Hart Publishing. pp. 1–38.

Exworthy T. (1995) Compulsory Care in the Community: A Review of the Proposals for Compulsory Supervision and Treatment of the Mentally Ill in the Community. *Criminal Behaviour and Mental Health*. **5**: 218–41.

Fennell P. (1991) Diversion of Mentally Disordered Offenders from Custody. *Criminal Law Review*. pp. 333–48.

Gostin L. (1983) The Ideology of Entitlement: the Application of Contemporary Legal Approaches to Psychiatry. In Bean P.T. (ed.) *Mental Illness: Changes and Trends*. John Wiley. pp. 27–54.

Gournay K., Sandford T., Johnson S. and Thornicroft G. (1997) Dual Diagnosis of Severe Mental Health Problems and Severe Abuse/Dependence: a Major Priority for Mental Health Nursing. *Journal of Psychiatric and Mental Health Nursing*. **4**: 89–95.

Grisso T. and Appelbaum P. (1998) *Assessing Competence to Consent to Treatment*. Oxford University Press.

Gronwell L. (1985) Legal Rights of the Mentally Ill. Judicial Situation. In Jensen K. and Pedersen B. (eds) *Commitment and Civil Rights of the Mentally Ill*. Sind Publications. pp. 254–8.

Grounds A. (1991) The Mentally Disordered in Prison. *Prison Service Journal*. **81** (Winter): 29–40.

Gunn J. (1977) Criminal Behaviour and Mental Disorder. *British Journal of Psychiatry*. **130** (April): 317–29.

Gunn J., Maden T. and Swinton M. (1991) *Mentally Disordered in Prison*. Report to the Home Office.

Harrison K. (1994) Supervision in the Community. *New Law Journal*. **144**: 1017.

Herridge C.F. (1989) Treatment of Psychotic Patients in Prison. (Letter) *Psychiatric Bulletin*. **13**(4): 200–1.

Hoggett B. (1984) (1996) *Mental Health Law*. Sweet & Maxwell. (2nd edn and 4th edn.)

Home Office (1990) *Provisions for the Mentally Disordered Offender*. Circular 66/90.

Home Office (1994) *Drug Misusers and the Criminal Justice System*. Part 2. *Police, Drug Misusers and the Community*. Report by the Advisory Council on the Misuse of Drugs. HMSO.

Hoyer G. (1999) On the Justification for Civil Commitment. (mimeo)

James A. (1996) *Life on the Edge* (Policy Report Vol. 1) Mental Health Foundation.

James D.V. and Hamilton L.W. (1991) The Clerkenwell Scheme: Assessing Efficacy and Cost of a Psychiatric Liaison Service to a Magistrates Court. *British Medical Journal*. **303**: 282–5 (3 August).

Jones H. (1992) *Revolving Doors. Report of the Telethon Inquiry into the Relationship between Mental Health, Homelessness and the Criminal Justice System*. NACRO.

Jones K. (1960) *Mental Health and Social Policy: 1854–1959*. Routledge & Kegan Paul.

Joseph P. (1992) *Psychiatric Assessment at the Magistrates Court*. Home Office/Department of Health.

Joseph P. and Potter M. (1990) Mentally Disordered Homelesss Offenders: Diversion from Custody. *Health Trends*. **22**: 51–3.

Kelly K., Bradshaw Y., Moon G. and Savage S. (1996) 'Doctored' Evidence; Care, Custody and the Forensic Medical Examiner. In Leishman F., Loveday B. and Savage S.P. *Core Issues in Policing*. Longman. pp. 160–74.

Kittrie N.N. (1971) *The Right to be Different*. Johns Hopkins Press.

Law Commission (1995) *Mental Incapacity*. Law Commission Report No. 231. HMSO.

Lewis P. (1980) *Psychiatric Probation Orders*. Institute of Criminology, Cambridge.

Macmillan Commission (1926) *Royal Commission on Lunacy and Mental Disorder*. Cmd. 2700. HMSO.

Matthews D., Ghodse A.H., Caan A.W. and Scott S.A. (1991) Cannabis Use in a Large Sample of Acute Psychiatric Admissions. *British Journal of Addiction*. **86** (June): 779–89.

Matthews E. (1999) Mental and Physical Illness; Unsustainable Seperation. In Eastman N. and Peay J. (eds) *Law without Enforcement*. Hart Publishing. pp. 47–58.

McConville M., Sanders A. and Leng R. (1991) *The Case for the Prosecution*. Routledge.

Menezes P.R., Johnson S. and Thornicroft G. (1996) Drug and Alcohol Problems among People with Severe Mental Illness in South London. *British Journal of Psychiatry*. **168**(5): 612–19.

Mental Health Act Commission. Biennial Reports (Fifth, Sixth, Seventh and Eighth Reports (1991–99)).

MIND (1993) *Diversion from Custody*. Information pack. MIND.

Morris N. (1980) Mental Illness and the Criminal Law. In Bean P.T. (ed.) *Mental Illness: Changes and Trends*. John Wiley. pp. 1–26.

Morris N. and Tonry M. (1990) *Between Prison and Probation: Intermediate Punishments in a Rational Sentencing System*. Oxford University Press.

NACRO (1993) *Diverting Mentally Disturbed Offenders from Prosecution*. (NACRO Mental Health Advisory Committee) Policy Paper 2. NACRO.

NACRO (1994) *Diverting Mentally Disturbed Offenders from Custodial Remands and Sentences*. (NACRO Mental Health Advisory Committee) Policy Paper 3. NACRO.

NHS Confederation (1999) *The Pocket Guide to the New NHS*. Merck Sharp and Dohme.

Negrete J.C., Knapp W.P. and Douglas D.E. (1986) Cannabis Affects the Severity of Schizophrenic Symptoms: Results of a Clinical Survey. *Psychological Medicine*. **16**: 515–20.

Nemitz T. (1997) The Use of the Appropriate Adult for Mentally Disordered Suspects in Police Stations. Unpublished PhD Thesis. University of Loughborough.

Nemitz T. and Bean P.T. (1995) Discrepancies and Inaccuracies in Statistics for Detained Patients. *Psychiatric Bulletin*. **19**(1): 28–32.

Peay J. (1993) A Criminological Perspective, The Influence of Fashion: a Theory on Practice and Disposal. Life chances in the Criminological Tombola. In Watson W. and Grounds A. (eds) *Mentally Disordered Offenders in an Era of Community Care*. Cambridge University Press.

Percy Commission (1957) *Royal Commission on the Law relating to Mental Illness and Mental Deficiency*. Cmnd. 169. HMSO.

Petersilia J. (1998) A Decade of Experimenting with Intermediate Sanctions: What Have We Learned? *Federal Probation*. **62**(2): 3–9.

Price C. and Caplan J. (1977) *The Confait Confessions*. Marion Boyars. London.

Prins H (1994) Is Diversion just a Diversion? *Medicine, Science and the Law.* **34**(2): 137–47.

Rassaby E. and Rogers A. (1987) Psychiatric Referrals from the Police: Variations in Disposal at Different Places of Safety. *Bulletin of the Royal College of Psychiatrists.* **11**(3): 78–81.

Regier D.A., Farmer M.E. and Rae D.S. (1990) Comorbidity of Mental Disorder with Alcohol and Other Drug Abuse: Results from ECA. *Journal of the American Medical Association.* **1264**(19): 2511–18.

Richardson G. (1999) *Draft Outline Proposals. Review of the Mental Health Act 1983*. Department of Health.

Ries R.R. (1993) The Dually Diagnosed Patient with Psychotic Symptoms. *Journal of Addictive Diseases.* **12**(2): 103–22.

Ries R. (1994) *Assessment and Treatment of Patients with Coexisting Mental Illness and Other Drug Abuse*. US Department of Health and Human Services.

Ritchie J.H., Dick D. and Lingham R. (1994) *Report of the Inquiry into the Care and Treament of Christopher Clunis* (The Ritchie Report). HMSO.

Rogers A. (1993) Police and Psychiatrists: a Case of Professional Dominance. *Social Policy and Administration.* **27**(15): 33–44.

Royal College of Psychiatrists (1987) Community Treatment Orders – A Discussion Document (April and October 1987). RCP.

Royal College of Psychiatrists (1996) *Report of the Confidential Inquiry into Homicides and Suicides by Mentally Disordered People*. RCP.

Royal Commission on Criminal Justice (1993) Chairman Lord Runciman. Cmd. 2263.

Royal Commission on Criminal Procedure (1981) *A Report*. HMSO.

Sainsbury Centre for Mental Health (1999) *A First Class Mental Health Service* and *NSF for Mental Health*. (Briefing Papers Nos 6 and 8). Sainsbury Centre for Mental Health.

Saloum I.S., Moss H.B. and Daly D.C. (1991) Substance Abuse and Schizophrenia. Impediments to Optimal Care. *American Journal of Alcohol Abuse.* **17**(3): 321–6.

Scott P.D. (1970) Punishment or Treatment. Prison or Hospital. *British Medical Journal.* (18 April) pp. 167–9.

Smith J. and Hucker S. (1994) Schizophrenia and Substance Abuse. *British Journal of Psychiatry.* **165**: 13–21.

Stark M.M. (1994) Management of Drug Users in Police Custody. *Journal of the Royal Society of Medicine.* **97**(Oct): 584–7.

Szasz T. (1983) Mental Illness as Strategy. In Bean P.T. (ed.) *Mental Illness: Changes and Trends*. John Wiley & Sons. pp. 93–114.

Turner W. and Tsuang M. (1990) The Impact of Substance Abuse on the Cause and Outcome of Schizophrenia. *Schizophrenia Bulletin.* **16**(1): 87–95.

Wexler D. and Winnick B. (1996) *Law in a Therapeutic Key*. Carolina Academic Press.

Index